Love-Based Copywriting Books

LOVE BASED COPYWRITING METHOD:

THE PHILOSOPHY BEHIND WRITING COPY THAT ATTRACTS, INSPIRES AND INVITES

LOVE-BASED COPYWRITING SYSTEM:

A STEP-BY-STEP PROCESS TO MASTER WRITING COPY THAT ATTRACTS, INSPIRES AND INVITES

by Michele PW (Michele Pariza Wacek)

This book may be purchased for educational, business, or sales promotional use. For information, please email info@michelepw.com.

ISBN 978-1-945363-16-0

Library of Congress Control Number: 2020939740

DEDICATION

I want to thank Nancy Marmolejo, Amethyst Wyldfyre and all the other conscious entrepreneurs who saw the vision of this book before I did (not to mention held my feet to the fire until I actually lived up to that vision).

Susan Liddy for giving me Love-Based — which was the final puzzle piece that allowed everything else to fall into place.

Christine Arylo for being my spiritual mentor and helping me clear the crap out of my head so I could finally start to truly come from love and abundance.

Andrea J. Lee for being my writer buddy and helping me stand into my vision.

Megan Yakovich for her wise and heartfelt editing.

Karin Wilson and Erin Ferree Stratton for providing the beautiful, visual design to bring these books into life.

And Paul for his love and support.

xxoo

Contents

Love-Based Copywriting Books

Dedication V

Book 1

LOVE BASED COPYWRITING METHOD: 1

THE PHILOSOPHY BEHIND WRITING COPYTHAT ATTRACTS,
INSPIRES AND INVITES 1

FOREWORD 3
by Susan Liddy, founder of the Love-Based Business Paradigm Movement 3

INTRODUCTION 5
WHY THIS BOOK? 5

CHAPTER 1 13
What Is Love-Based Copy? 13

CHAPTER 2 27
IT ALL STARTS WITH WORDS 27

CHAPTER 3 37
Ideal Clients 37
Exercise 44

CHAPTER 4. 47

Pain Versus Pleasure 47

Exercise 55

CHAPTER 5. 57

What Is YOUR "Come From" When You Market?. 57

CHAPTER 6. 67

The Philosophy Behind Selling in a Love-Based Way 67

CHAPTER 7. 81

Choose Love-Based Triggers Versus Fear-Based Triggers 81

Urgency as a Trigger: 81

You Can Also Combine Pain and Urgency: 83

Using Pleasure as a Trigger:. 84

Not Using Exaggeration As A Trigger: 85

"Unselling" as a Trigger:. 85

CHAPTER 8. 89

Pulling it All Together 89

LOVE-BASED COPYWRITING SYSTEM: 93

A STEP-BY-STEP PROCESS TO MASTER WRITING COPY THAT
ATTRACTS, INSPIRES AND INVITES. 93

INTRODUCTION — 1

Why Love-Based Copy? 1

HOW TO BEST USE THIS BOOK 5

WHAT TO DO BEFORETHE WRITING STARTS. 9

CHAPTER 1. 11
Your Pre-Writing Checklist 11
EXERCISE 13
EXERCISE 16
Facing the Blank Page. 23

WHERE THE WRITING HAPPENS. 29

CHAPTER 3. 31
Headlines 31
Prehead: 34
Headline: 36
Subheads: 38
Exercise 39
Love-Based Tip: Don't exaggerate. 41

CHAPTER 4. 43
Beginnings 43
Exercise 47
Love-Based Tips: Writing a Powerful Beginning. 48
Your Million-Dollar Story. 51
Exercise 56
Love-Based Tip: Don't Be Afraid to Be Vulnerable 58

CHAPTER 6. 61
Your Solution:The Big Picture Overview. 61
Exercise 67
Love-Based Tip: Stick with What Works 69

CHAPTER 7. 71
Your Solution: Drilling Down Into the Details 71

Exercise 78

Love-Based Tip: Amplify Emotions, Not Pain 82

Packaging Your Genius (i.e. Your Love-Based Offer) 85

OVERVIEW OF TRANSFORMATION(covered in detail in Chapter 6): 86

Service Delivery: 87

Bonuses: 88

Cost/ Justify Cost: 90

Guarantee: 92

Call to action: 94

Exercise 95

Love-Based Tip:Make Peace with Money. 96

CHAPTER 9. 99

Objections 99

Example of Frequently Asked Question section: 107

Exercise 108

Love-Based Tip: Give Your Ideal Clients Space. 109

CHAPTER 10. 113

What Else Do You Need? Other Essential Elements to Complete Your Marketing Pieces 113

Exercise 119

Love-Based Tip: Watch the Hype. 121

PUTTING IT ALL TOGETHER 123

CHAPTER 11. 125

Applying the System to Emails, Sales Letters, Opt-In Pages, Websites and Direct Mail 125

CHAPTER 12 — ADVANCED TIPS 141

CHAPTER 13 — WHAT'S NEXT? 151

APPENDIX — IMPROVE YOUR WRITING VOICE 153

5 Ways to Add Your Personality toYour Writing 153

3 Tips to Improve Your Writing Rhythm 156

Writing Exercises — Get in Touch with Your Writing Rhythm. . . . 159

ABOUT THE AUTHOR **161**

ABOUT MICHELE PW 161

RESOURCES **163**

OTHER BOOKS IN THE LOVE-BASED BUSINESS SERIES **164**

We would be happy to write your copy for you!. 170

Done-For-You Copywriting Services — Get More Leads, Clients and Sales WITHOUT Doing the Work Yourself! 170

Testimonials 172

Books 1 & 2

Book 1

LOVE BASED COPYWRITING METHOD:

THE PHILOSOPHY BEHIND WRITING COPY
THAT ATTRACTS, INSPIRES AND INVITES

Foreword

BY SUSAN LIDDY, FOUNDER OF THE LOVE-BASED BUSINESS PARADIGM MOVEMENT

As a consumer, I always hated marketing and advertising.

I hated how they triggered my fears, made me feel less than incapable and tried to manipulate me into the sale.

So, of course, one of the first things I noticed when I entered the business world as a business owner was how much fear was rooted in the coaching industry. Pretty much all the marketing, sales and copywriting was fear-based.

The last thing I wanted to do was dump more fear-based marketing messages into the world, so I started to search for a better way. Unfortunately, all I found were "gurus" who were actively teaching and encouraging the use of the tactics that I deplored.

At first I despaired. Until I realized I was the one who was meant to step up and be that expert in the Love-Based Business Paradigm.

As time went on, though, I've come to realize an even deeper message. I see now that while I was meant to give birth to the Love-Based Business Paradigm, I was not meant to nurture and grow it by myself. The Love-Based Business Paradigm

3

needs a bigger platform than what I can do by myself as an entrepreneur.

It needs to be a movement.

They say that it takes a village to raise a child, and it most certainly takes a village to raise a movement. To honor that, I invite all coaches and service-based business owners to use their version of Love-Based Business and spread the movement far and wide. Together, we can change how marketing and advertising is being done.

Michele PW is a gifted copywriter who knows and understands love-based copywriting inside and out. She has done incredible work for me and my business and I am honored that she is taking the lead in bringing love-based copywriting front and center with this book that you now hold in your hands.

With all my love.

Susan Liddy

Author of "Love-Based Marketing: The No Sell-Out, Copy-Out, Burn-Out Method to Attract Your Soul Mate Clients into Your Business" www.SusanLiddy.com

Introduction
WHY THIS BOOK?

I've wanted to write this book for a good long time, even if I didn't fully realize it until recently.

As a child (3 years old), I taught myself to read because I wanted to write stories so badly.

As a teenager, I tried to figure out what to do to make money while I wrote my novels. Everyone said I should be a journalist, but that was the last thing I wanted to be.

Instead, while in college, I discovered the wonderful world of copywriting.

Copywriting, which has nothing to do with protecting intellectual property or putting a copyright on something, is all about writing promotional materials for businesses. Businesses have a lot of copy they need written, but rather than hire a lot of employees to get it all done, they use freelancers. Hence, there's an entire freelance copywriting industry out there devoted to serving those businesses.

For years, I bounced between freelancing and working full time (which included freelancing as I was working) until 1998 when I quit my job to pursue full-time copywriting.

Along the way, I discovered I had a talent for not only writing promotional copy, but also for crafting marketing strategy. I also discovered I was most passionate and excited when I was working on campaigns that directly resulted in my clients growing their businesses. Put those two together, and it made sense for me to stop being a generic copywriter who would write anything (and as a side note, being a generalist is NOT a great business model) and instead specialize in direct response copy and marketing.

Direct response copy is actually a subset of copywriting. It's a specialized form of writing copy where folks are directly responding to the marketing piece by taking action. That action could be anything from clicking a link in an email to exchanging a name and email for access to a training call to buying a product. (Other examples of traditional direct response include infomercials and junk mail — and if you're like most folks, the term "junk mail" doesn't evoke fuzzy hearts and rainbows type feelings. Traditional direct response copy like this HAS gotten a bad rap - more to come on this, below.)

Because direct response copy does a lot of heavy lifting for the business owner or entrepreneur, it's actually an extremely powerful tool to have in your toolbox. When you master this skill, you have the power to simply send an email and watch sales come in.

So, it sounds like a no-brainer to use direct response copy in your business. Right?

Well…

Have you ever been reading an online sales letter, and as you scroll down looking for the price (all the while wondering if anyone actually reads these things), you can't help but feel like the copy is hype-y, sales-y, and inauthentic?

If you're an entrepreneur or a business owner, have you ever consequently cringed at the thought of using direct response copy in your own business?

These feelings are likely amplified if you consider yourself "conscious" or "heart-centered" or "spiritual" or "transformational" or "creative." You may even feel completely out of integrity at the thought of using a tool in your business that feels so inauthentic.

Worse, if you've ever tried to tell the "gurus" how you don't want to use direct response copy because of how it makes you feel when you read it – that you want an alternative - you may have basically been told to quit bellyaching and pull up your "big girl" or "big boy" panties. After all, you WANT to make money from your marketing materials, don't you?

I know this happens, because a lot of my friends and clients in the transformational industry have experienced it. That's why they encouraged me to come up with a new way to write copy that didn't feel so "icky." They proposed names like "conscious" copywriting or "attraction" copywriting, but that didn't feel right to me. I didn't necessarily want to create an alternative way to write copy (which could be considered "less than" traditional direct response copywriting — "if you're not a REAL business owner, you can go use that attraction copywriting, but if you're serious about your business, you'll buckle down and use grown-up direct response copywriting").

What I wanted to do was transform the entire direct response copywriting industry. I just didn't know how.

And then my friend Susan Liddy came into my life (you can read more about her in the Foreword, if you haven't already).

Susan wrote a book titled "Love-Based Marketing: The No Sell-Out, Copy-Out, Burn-Out Method to Attract Your Soul Mate Clients into Your Business." Basically, she wanted to offer an alternative to marketing that was based in love, rather than fear.

Hmmm.

That's when it hit me: could this be what was happening with that "icky-feeling" copywriting, too?

Is traditional copywriting based in fear?

And then the epiphany: what if we wrote copy based in love?

Love-based copywriting.

That's when all the pieces fell into place.

I published my first Love-Based Copywriting book in August, 2014. I called it "Love-Based Copywriting: How to Write Copy That Attracts, Inspires and Invites Your Ideal Prospects to Become Ideal Clients." And it was a huge hit.

I had entrepreneurs reach out to me everywhere in the world to tell me how this book completely transformed their business. It gave them a sense of peace that nothing else ever had.

So my mission was clear. I needed to get the word out about love-based copywriting.

I spent a year promoting it — writing articles, blog posts and getting on dozens of radio shows, podcasts and live stages to spread the word. And along the way, I became even clearer about what love-based copy is, and the philosophy behind it.

And somewhere along the way, I realized that first book needed an upgrade. There was more I needed to say about the philosophy behind writing love-based copy.

With the new edition came a new title, too — "Love-Based Copywriting Method: The Philosophy Behind Writing Copy

That Attracts, Inspires and Invites" (which is the book you now hold in your hand).

(Another side note here — sometimes getting your work out there, even if you later realize it's not as perfect as it could be, is the best thing you can do. Only by talking about the book to other people and getting their feedback and questions was I able to see what I needed to do to make the book stronger.)

I also realized I needed a second Love-Based Copywriting book, which would focus more on the "how-to" when it comes to writing love-based copy. It needed to teach all the specific nuts and bolts involved, such as writing headlines, features and benefits and more.

So, I also wrote a second book — "Love-Based Copywriting System: A Step-by-Step Process to Master Writing Copy That Attracts, Inspires and Invites."

While the two books are magic together, they also stand well on their own.

So, if you are looking to learn the philosophy around writing love-based copy, including how to emotionally connect with your ideal clients using psychological triggers (or hot buttons) in a love-based way, this book is for you. It doesn't matter if you're a beginner or advanced entrepreneur; if being love-based in your copy and/or marketing is important to you, this book can help you accomplish that.

If you're interested in writing your own love-based copy, after reading this one about the philosophy behind it, then my "Love-Based Copywriting System" is also for you. (You can learn more here: www.LoveBasedCopyBooks.com.)

How to Use This Book

Even though this book doesn't get into the nuts and bolts of actually writing copy, you'll still find a lot of exercises and strategies to help you integrate the love-based philosophy into your marketing and copy.

I start by describing the basics, so you get the foundation - the love-based copy principles. Once you have a clear understanding of what love-based copy is (and how it compares to fear-based), then I move into exercises, so you can start implementing those principles into your business.

In the Resources section, I provide additional supporting materials plus next steps, depending on where you are in your business and where you want to go next.

And, if at any time, you decide the last thing you want to do is write your own copy, we'd love to do it for you. You can learn more about our services at www.MichelePW.com/services.

Chapter 1
WHAT IS LOVE-BASED COPY?

Before you can fully understand the concept of love-based copy, you need to clearly understand direct response copywriting.

There are actually 2 things to consider here.

On the surface, direct response copy is writing promotional materials that get people to take action — to directly respond to the written material. (Remember, this has nothing to do with putting a copyright on something or protecting your intellectual property.)

But what direct response copywriting REALLY is, above all else, is leverage and freedom. Good direct response copy will do a lot of the heavy lifting for you – that's the leverage part. It will allow you to market and sell one-to-many versus one-to-one.

You see, if you aren't using direct response marketing and copy in your biz, then chances are your sales and marketing activities look something like this:

- You go out and hustle up some prospects by networking (online or offline) and talking to folks.

- You follow up with them one-on-one, with calls and emails.

13

💜 You meet with them again, and have a sales conversation.

💜 You personally continue to follow up with them (again and again) until they say either "yes" or "no."

Now, when you use direct response copy in your biz, all that changes:

💜 The copy can attract your ideal prospects.

💜 The copy can follow up with your ideal prospects.

💜 The copy can invite/have sales conversations with your ideal prospects.

💜 The copy can follow up until they say "yes" or "no."

Do you see how much easier marketing your biz becomes?

And even if you DO need to have a conversation to complete the sales process with a prospect, chances are the prospect will be pretty close to making a decision already, so he or she only needs a few questions answered. This means your sales calls are also much shorter.

Because direct response copy has the ability to do so much on its own, you can essentially automate your sales and marketing processes. And that's why it's at the heart of all those claims to making money on the Internet. (You know what I'm talking about — make money in your sleep, work from home in your PJs for a few hours a day and make hundreds or even thousands of dollars, etc. Of course, while there CAN be some "truth" to that claim — the REAL story is there's still a lot of hard work and long hours before you even get within shouting distance of that reality. But that's a different book for a different time.)

This is why, if you are an entrepreneur, implementing direct response copy in your biz is critical. It's how you can have a bigger reach AND enjoy more freedom. Without it, your precious time is already stretched to the limit, and your ability to get your message and gifts out into the world is severely hampered. Even if you have a strong team supporting you, you still can't replace the role direct response copy can fill in your biz.

So how can direct response possibly do all of this? Is it magic? Does it have secret powers?

No, it's not magic, even if it sometimes feels like it.

There are a couple of reasons direct response copywriting works. First, it triggers emotions in the reader, which causes them to take action (i.e. buy something). In fact, in a lot of cases it mimics our psychological buying process — the act of buying is, first and foremost, an emotional process. (We're going to get into this a lot more in the following chapters; this is just to give you a little background info.)

Basically, all emotions can be broken down into two main categories — love and fear. Love-based emotions include love, hope, gratitude, joy, connection, inspiration, peace, and respect. Fear-based emotions include fear, anger, grief, shame, guilt, blame, worry, and anxiety.

Now, the thing about fear-based emotions is they feel, well, BAD. They're uncomfortable and unpleasant, and we typically want to stop feeling them as quickly as possible.

Which is why they work so well to compel people to take action.

You see, if you stir up fear-based emotions in people, and then tell them if they take X action, those fear-based emotions will go away, then a lot of times people will take that action. It doesn't matter if you're trying to persuade people to floss more or get your kids to behave or sell a product to your ideal clients — if you trigger fear-based emotions in people, and then tell them the solution to stop feeling that emotion is to take action, in many cases they'll take the action. They just want to move away from the pain.

(There's a dirty little secret that comes with that though — the fear-based emotion doesn't actually go away with the action. It just gets buried or pushed away or numbed, which is why using fear to persuade isn't a lasting or permanent solution. I'll dig into this more later in the book.)

Now, remember, buying is an emotional process. So you DO need to trigger emotions in your ideal clients. And how do you do that? By using something called "triggers" or "psychological triggers," which are basically designed to push people's hot buttons.

These triggers have been around since we were all living in caves and running away from the saber-toothed tiger, which means they're buried deep in our psyche, and in many cases are directly connected to our survival instincts.

Triggers include:

- Finding love/a relationship

- Sex appeal

- Having enough food, warmth, shelter, etc.

- Making sure our children are taken care of

- Knowing we'll be taken care of in our old age

- Being part of a community

Now, because these are connected to our survival instincts, in many cases our FEAR of losing them is stronger than our DESIRE to move toward them.

This is one of the reasons why creating fear is EASIER than creating love. (I'll get into this more later in the book, too.)

So, let's look at how you would use fear-based emotional triggers in a buying situation.

First, the fear is stirred up or agitated. The sales person tries to make the person feel as badly as possible about their current situation. After they feel pretty bad, then the sales person brings in love-based emotions as the solution.

Because, you see, what people WANT to feel are those love-based emotions. They WANT hope and transformation. People WANT to buy — they just don't want to be sold to. (Buying is fun, being sold to is not.)

So, in many traditional selling situations, sales people have mixed love and fear together. The problem is, the moment you access the fear (even if the conversation or process is, let's say, only based in about ten percent fear), the entire process will reek of fear.

And this is why so many folks are turned off by sales.

So what does this have to do with direct response copy? Well, remember, direct response copy is a way to sell one-to-many, so it makes sense that it would take a lot of its structure from good ol' selling skills. (This is why you may have heard the phrase "copywriting is salesmanship in print.") This is also why plenty of good or even excellent writers can't write a direct response page that gets results (because they lack sales skills). It's also why average or even below average writers who have strong sales skills can still get pretty decent results.

Now, that said, I want to stress (and this is REALLY important) that there is a difference between fear and pain. A lot of times fear is imaginary — but pain is not. People are in pain all the time. YOUR ideal prospects are in pain right now, and they need your gift or message to get out of it. Reminding them of their pain in order to give them the motivation to take action and get out of that pain is a gift. Scaring them because you want their money is what makes things feel "icky," and it's how direct response copy got its bad rap in the first place. (More on pain vs. pleasure later in the book.)

Now, if you're wondering how fear shows up in copy, here are a few examples of fear-based copy:

Example 1

> "You're going to have a stroke or a heart attack if you don't lose some weight."

That's what the nurse told me.

Then I eliminated this ONE food from my diet... and lost 91 pounds of fat WITHOUT "dieting" or "exercising."

You're probably eating this so-called "health food" every day, so please click the link below to read this life-saving health message now, before it's too late:

Example 2

I can't believe you still haven't activated your VIP $500-day-software we set-up for you last week... Really??

Click here to activate it now so you can finally start making some decent profits online...

Please don't put this off again. It just breaks my heart to bring something valuable to you and you just ignore it...

Are you not interested anymore?

Go here now to let me know YES or NO.

Example 3

(This last example isn't technically fear-based as it's not tapping into fear, but it is an example of the exaggeration that's so prevalent in fear-based copywriting.)

> My name is Lisa and I found the solution to dropping 17 lbs in ONE WEEK.
>
> I know this sounds like a gimmick. It isn't.
>
> In 7 short days, I was able to transform my body:
>
> → My hips went from 41" to 36"
>
> → My waist went from 34" to 30"
>
> → My body fat went from 38% down to 30%

You can feel the fear and exaggeration, right? And how does it feel? Yucky, right?

It probably makes you want to do something, anything to alleviate the fear. Like for instance — buy a product.

Poof! And that, my friends, is how direct response copy became the backbone of Internet Marketing - and ALSO how it's gotten its less-than-stellar reputation.

Because triggering fear is easier than triggering love, a lot of marketers resort to triggering fear in order to make money quickly. (While this can work in the short-term, in the long-term it can damage your brand, your reputation, your integrity and overall, your biz. More on this later.)

So rather than viewing direct response copywriting as a way to leverage yourself and your marketing so you can make a bigger impact in the world and help the people you're meant to help (which it absolutely CAN do), it's regarded as something sort of shady — full of hype and slime. It becomes something best left in the shadows of your biz. And really, something any reputable (and especially conscious or heart-centered) entrepreneur wants no part of.

Now, in my eBook, "The Dirty Little Secret About Direct Response/Internet Marketing: Why What You've Been Taught Isn't Working for You and What You Can Do to Turn it Around," I talk more about how direct response copywriting became so prevalent on the Internet and also why it triggers a negative reaction in so many entrepreneurs who consider themselves "mission driven" or "creative" or "agents of change." (You can check it out here at LoveBasedCopyBooks. com). But in a nutshell, two of the biggest reasons why entrepreneurs struggle with direct response copy are:

- It closely mimics selling skills (in other words, if you hate to sell – and a lot of conscious entrepreneurs do — you probably hate direct response copy).

- It focuses on fear, which is not in integrity with your core message that is typically around hope and love.

22

The selling part isn't going to change (sorry guys). Unfortunately, if you are a conscious entrepreneur and you hate to sell, this IS something you're going to have to come to terms with if you want to have a successful, profitable business that actually reaches everyone you know you're meant to reach. (HOWEVER, reading this book CAN help you with that — in fact, I have a whole section dedicated to why it's a disservice NOT to sell later in the book. The more comfortable you are with selling, the more comfortable you'll be with direct response copy.)

BUT, the second part absolutely CAN change — we CAN base direct response copy around love instead of fear. And once we do that, our resistance to selling may diminish, as well.

So what IS love-based copywriting?

Love-based copywriting still uses triggers, because you need the triggers to inspire people to take action. But rather than using triggers to make people feel fear, shame, guilt or create a false sense of urgency (which is what fear-based copywriting does), you create a buying environment that attracts and invites your ideal, perfect clients to say YES to moving forward with you.

Now, the problem with love-based copywriting is it may not be as immediately effective as fear-based. It's possible (but NOT a given) that you would make more sales using fear-based than love-based copy. But while you may make more money in the short-term, in the long-term you run the risk of eroding your business. People don't like feeling the way fear-based copywriting makes them feel, so there could be a backlash to your brand. Also, if people are buying in reaction to painful emotions, you could end up attracting the wrong clients, which is just about the last thing you want to do, because clients who are wrong for you will probably take more of your time and energy to make happy, and after all of that, they STILL won't be happy and may refund and/or tell people they had a bad experience with you (which can also impact future sales).

So to sum it up — when you use fear-based copywriting, you MAY make more sales, but you also may end up with a higher percentage of refunds and unhappy clients, not to mention experiencing a slow erosion of your brand.

With love-based copywriting, you MAY make less overall sales, but you're far more likely to attract the perfect people into your programs, who will be a joy to work with, who will do everything you say, experience huge transformation, and become your raving fans.

And that's not all! Love-based copywriting also has the power to grow your brand in a more powerful way.

(Doesn't that feel just so yummy perfect?)

So if you're ready to become part of the transformation of direct response copywriting ... if you're ready to learn how to use love and respect to increase your reach and visibility while growing your business, keep reading! Because the exciting news is you absolutely CAN. And this book is going to show you how.

Chapter 2
IT ALL STARTS WITH WORDS

When you're sitting down to write love-based copy, one of the most crucial elements is making sure you mindset or "come from" is aligned with love and abundance. I devote an entire chapter to this later in the book, but for right now I want to cover Internet Marketing vocabulary, because understanding the terminology is an important first step.

As traditional sales and marketing relies on tapping into fear-based emotions, there are a lot of "dehumanizing" words associated with it — "leads," "squeeze pages," "list," etc. And, when you think about it, it makes sense. If you're going to purposely trigger fear-based emotions in your customers in order to compel them to buy, you really don't want to consider what you're doing to actual human beings.

Now, I want to stress, I don't think this was done intentionally nor do I think anyone is "bad" for doing it. I go into more detail around the "why folks market this way" later in the book.

But, as we move into the love-based philosophy, we want to be mindful about our own mindset and actions, and changing our own language around common Internet Marketing terms is a great first step to help you move into that space of love and abundance.

So without further ado, let's jump in.

Website — So the "official" definition is a collection of web pages that lives on the Internet and provides a broad overview of your business.

However, here in love-based copywriting land, we shift that definition a bit. Here, a website is an "online showroom."

If you had a "bricks and mortar" business, you would have a showroom where you could invite your ideal prospects to sit down, have a cup of tea and talk about how your biz could help them solve what's keeping them up at night. Right?

Well, your "online showroom" serves the exact same purpose. Your website is essentially an invitation to your ideal prospects to stop in for a cup of tea and a chat to see if what you sell is the perfect fit for what they are looking for.

(And yes, it really IS a 2-way conversation — as your ideal prospects read, they're having a conversation in their head with your copy, and if they decide they're done, the conversation is over.)

Branding/Taglines/Logos — I define branding as the overall feeling people have around your business, which is usually based on their experience with it. It includes things like (but is not limited to) logos and taglines. Logos are graphical representations of your business while taglines are brief word descriptions.

I know lots of entrepreneurs get hung up on taglines and logos, and while having both is never a bad idea since they can certainly help your business (I personally have a logo I love — my exclamation point) they aren't necessary to actually making money. If you're just starting out, I wouldn't worry much about a logo or tagline. Instead, I'd focus more on other direct response pieces (such as a really good opt-in page and freebie — see below) to start building my community and making money.

Sales Letters (also known as long-copy sales letters or long-form sales letters) — These are the super-long pages on the Internet where you scroll down for what seems like forever looking for a price.

Now, in the land of love-based copywriting, I want you to think about these online sales letters as "departments" in your online showroom, because these pages are how you sell specific products, programs, events, etc.

Emails — Emails (or electronic mail) can be used for all sorts of things — staying in touch with old friends, communicating with clients, or marketing to your ideal prospects. In love-based copywriting, I like to think of emails as sales representatives who direct your ideal prospects to the perfect department (i.e. sales letter) for them.

Opt-in Page/Landing Page/Squeeze Page — All of these titles refer to the exact same thing: a page that asks for a name and email in exchange for something free. If you're offering a free call or webinar, or a special report pdf, or a recording of a training (or any other type of free offer), you would likely use an opt-in page to collect information.

Here in love-based copywriting land, I prefer the term "opt-in page" (which is the term we'll use throughout this book) because it best reflects the actual process: your ideal prospects choose to give you their contact info and start a relationship with you. ("Squeeze page" in particular is a very manipulative term, as it refers to the page "squeezing" the contact information out of people.) I also like to think of opt-in pages as the "line outside your online showroom."

Ideal Clients/Ideal Prospects — This one is so important I've devoted the next chapter entirely to how to find your ideal clients, but I wanted to at least get the conversation started with a quick definition. Here in the land of love-based copywriting, we prefer the terms "ideal clients" for customers and "ideal prospects" for leads.

I don't like "leads" because it depersonalizes your prospects — and once you've depersonalized your prospects, it's not a leap to then depersonalize your customers. You might even start thinking of them as "walking wallets." (And once you start thinking about your customers as "walking wallets," it's a lot easier to use fear-based direct response tactics since you're only thinking about trying to squeeze as much money out of them as you can — you don't really care about how they feel.)

The term "customers" doesn't really bother me, but I think it's more powerful to get into the habit of calling your customers "ideal clients" or "ideal customers," because it's actually a lot easier to write copy and create marketing campaigns that attract your ideal clients versus attracting just anyone who is willing to pay you money regardless of whether or not he/she is a good fit for you and your business. (Yes! It really is! Keep reading to find out why and how.)

Community/List – "List" is an old term, which basically refers to a list of folks you can contact — in many cases it's a list of email addresses. Since so much of online marketing depends on sending emails, the more email addresses you have (i.e. the bigger list), the more desirable of a joint venture or affiliate partner you are. (Joint venture and affiliates are folks who promote your products and services and you pay them a commission for every sale that comes out of their promotion. The difference between joint venture and affiliates typically is the level of promotion and commitment — joint venture partners typically act more like actual partners, and the two of you will work harder to promote each other to your respective communities, whereas affiliates are typically less committed to you and the promotion.)

Now I don't like "list," because it also depersonalizes your ideal prospects. All of a sudden they are reduced to an email address — not living, breathing people. That's why I like "community."

Plus, "community" is all-encompassing. Your promotional efforts can be much bigger than simply a list of emails you have permission to mail to. Your community includes your Twitter and Facebook friends, blog readers, podcast listeners, video watchers, etc. Really, anyone who is following you (no matter what medium they choose) is part of your community.

Conversions — The holy grail of direct response — direct response copy lives and dies by conversion rate. Conversion rate refers to the percentage of folks who read your copy and take the desired action (ie. how many visitors to your website give you their email address, how many people who read your sales letter buy your product, etc.). Conversion rates vary depending upon what you're asking people to do (i.e. click on a link in an email, give you their email address or get out their credit card to buy something). For instance, a good conversion rate for a sales letter is 1% — that means 1 out of every 100 people who visit your sales letter buy.

If you're asking folks to do something that's free (i.e. give you their email address in exchange for something like a special report or webinar) you should have a higher conversion rate than 1%, but there's a huge variation because there are so many other factors. In some cases, you might see 20%-30% conversions on opt-ins (i.e. using a paid Facebook ad campaign that sends new "colder" visitors to your website, who may never have heard of you before so they may be less likely to opt-in for your freebie) to 60% or higher (i.e. having an affiliate/JV partner send an email to their list or you send an email to your list to an opt-in page, because the people who click on those links are much warmer as they would have some sort of relationship with you or your affiliate/JV partner, so they are more likely to opt-in).

Headlines — The big words at the top of the page. On "Planet Direct Response Copywriting," the point of the headline is to get folks to start reading the copy. That's it. (And that's actually a pretty big job as typically 80% of the people who end up reading copy say they based their decision to start reading on the headline.)

Because headlines are so critical to the success of a direct response piece (as you can imagine, it's tough to get someone to do something if they don't read anything) headlines are one of the first things people test when they're trying to improve conversions.

In addition to headlines, there are also pre-heads (you can find pre-heads above the headlines, typically they're in a smaller font and they may also be highlighted) and subheads (these are found below the headline and also can be used to break up longer pieces of copy).

Call to Action (CTA) — Just as you always find headlines at the top of a piece of copy, a call to action is found at the bottom. A call to action is exactly that — you're making a call for people to take your desired action. It could be to buy something, it could be to send an email, it could be to fill out a form, it could be to click on a link or give you an email address, etc. There are lots and lots of different types of CTAs, but the most important thing to remember is you MUST include one if you're writing direct response copy.

Features/Benefits — So it's important to begin a piece of copy with a headline and end it with a CTA, but what about the muddy middle? Ah, that's where features and benefits come in.

You use features and benefits to describe your product/service/ program/etc. Features are the service delivery – what you're actually selling. Is it a book? A CD set? An event? A coaching program?

Now, while people DO need to know what they're buying, they aren't really buying a bunch of CDs or a chance to yak with you on the phone. What they're really buying is the outcome, the transformation, the solution to their problem. So you need to describe what you're selling to your ideal clients in a way that clearly explains "what's in it for them." This is what is known as benefits.

90% of the description of your product should be about the benefits, and 10% should be about the features. What typically happens when entrepreneurs are first starting out is that 90%

of the description is around the features and 10% is around the benefits. Even seasoned entrepreneurs (who really ought to know better) struggle with this, so you're not alone if this doesn't come as easily to you as you'd like.

Why? Well I think it's a couple of things. First, as the creator of the product/program/service, you are far more focused on the features than the benefits, so that's what pops up first in your head. (Especially if this is a product that's taken awhile to actually birth — the more time you spent on it, the more you want people to know how involved and in-depth it is.) Second, it's definitely a lot easier to write features than benefits – the features merely describe what people actually get (remember – a book / CD / program). Benefits require you to dig deeper – to get under the surface and at the heart of WHY someone should spend their hard-earned money to buy your offering. That takes more work than simply describing what the program is. Note — if you are looking for more "nuts and bolts" copywriting teaching, make sure you check out Volume 2 of my Love-Based Business series: "The Love-Based Copywriting System." That's where I go into much more detail about how to actually write headlines, calls to action, features/benefits and the other essential direct response copy elements.

So that covers basic copywriting terms. Let's move on to the heart of what puts the "love" in love-based copywriting,

starting with ideal clients.

Chapter 3
IDEAL CLIENTS

Knowing who your ideal clients are is not only critical to writing love-based copy, but also to building a successful, profitable, love-based business. This is why I've devoted an entire chapter to finding and understanding your ideal client.

Let's start by talking about what makes ideal clients different from target markets or niche markets. Target markets (the customers your business serves) typically are more demographically based — for instance, your target market may be stay-at-home moms between the ages of 30 and 50.

Niche markets take target markets one step further by refining and specializing who you're selling to. A niche market may be stay-at-home moms, between the ages of 30 and 50, who are looking for a home-based business opportunity.

The reason a lot of marketers recommend "niche-ing" down your target market is because the more focused you are when it comes to who you're selling to, the easier it is to sell to them. If everyone you're selling to has some common ground you can speak to, the easier it is to market and sell to them, because you can emphasize that common ground. In addition, even though it sounds counter-intuitive, when you try to sell to everyone, you actually end up selling to nobody. Why? Well a couple of reasons.

First, if you're trying to sell to everyone, you're probably getting pretty generic. And the more generic you get, the less people are going to recognize their SPECIFIC problem in your generic description. Remember, your ideal clients live in a world of specifics — their problem is very real and very specific to them. In fact, they may even go as far as to say "but MY situation/problem is different/unique etc." They only see what makes them unique, not what they have in common with others who have their same problem.

That's why if you are equally specific, they'll recognize themselves in your copy and think "Wow, I can see myself here," or "She's really talking to me." If you stay in the land of generalities, you run the very real risk of them walking right by your marketing materials, because they don't recognize themselves or their problem in them.

In addition, when people are ready to solve a problem, they tend to (but not always) want to hire a specialist. Because once they've decided they're ready to get rid of the problem, they don't want to waste their time and money on something that may not work for them (and when things are generic, they don't always work for specific cases, especially if those specific cases are more complicated or difficult than generic cases.). So they're going to, as much as possible, try and work with the specialist, so they can finally solve those problems once and for all.

Now, while I agree with the concept of niche markets, I don't like niche markets alone because I don't think they go deep enough. That's where the concept of ideal client comes in.

You see, the problem with niche markets and target markets is they're based too much on external factors — i.e. demographic info. Ideal clients, on the other hand, are defined by internal factors — values, motivations, and core beliefs.

The more you can tune into what's going on in your clients' head, the easier it will be to attract them, because they'll feel like you really "get" them. Also, knowing who your ideal clients are and specifically writing to them in your copy is one of the key principles of writing love-based copy.

So what does focusing on internal factors mean, exactly? Well, remember my niche market example — stay-at-home moms looking for a home-based business opportunity? There are actually two ideal client groups in that one niche market.

The first ideal client group consists of mothers who are looking for a biz opportunity because they want something for themselves. They feel like their entire lives are wrapped around taking care of other people and that they're losing their identity as a person. Their financial needs are met, so they don't necessarily need the income (although they may want the income) but mostly what they're looking for is something just for them.

Now, just because they're looking for something for themselves doesn't mean they want to ignore their family. Au Contraire — being there for their family is very important, so this biz opportunity must be flexible. They need to be able to do it when they can fit it into their busy lives. They still want to cook dinner and cheer at soccer games and pick up the dry cleaning. So this business opportunity needs to fit into the open time pockets they have throughout their days.

Okay so that's ideal client group 1. Ideal client group 2 consists of moms who have found themselves in a situation where they need to be the bread winner. They are looking for a biz opportunity that will pay the mortgage and put food on the table, and they want that to happen as fast as possible. While having a flexible work schedule is nice, they don't necessarily mind putting in long hours if they'll be able to support their family. So for them, what's most important is how much money they can make with this biz opportunity.

So think about these two ideal client groups. Do you see how different they are? And do you see how different the messages to each of them would need to be? (Ideal client 1 would be all about flexibility and having something for herself while ideal client 2 would be all about how much and how fast she can make money.) Yet on the surface they're in the same niche market. That's why taking that next step and moving from niche markets to ideal client is so crucial.

Now, you may be thinking — why do I have to make a choice? Why can't I put BOTH messages into my copy?

Well, the problem is if you try to talk to both groups, you'll likely talk to neither. Because ideal client 1 is not motivated by money, any messages about money wouldn't land for her. She might feel like the biz opportunity wouldn't be all that flexible after all and she would have to compromise her family duties. And ideal client 2 may read about the flexibility and be concerned she won't make the money she needs to make after all, and look elsewhere.

Think about yourself as a consumer. When you're looking for a product or service to solve a problem you have, you want it to be as specific to your problem as possible, right? Likely you aren't looking for a general solution because a general solution may not solve your SPECIFIC problem — and you don't want to spend the time or money screwing around with something that won't actually take care of your problem.

That's what your ideal clients will feel if they read too many messages in your copy — even if your solution really CAN solve the problems of multiple people, they may just not believe it. (Or, what they likely will believe is your solution can solve OTHER people's problems, just not THEIR SPECIFIC problems.)

Now, one reason entrepreneurs want to have multiple messages in their copy is because they're worried their ideal client group is too small. What if they don't have enough clients? What if they end up turning good-paying clients away?

Those fears are completely normal and natural, so let's talk about why attracting ideal clients will actually make your business more profitable (not to mention enjoyable) than selling to anyone and everyone.

1. You actually will attract more clients being more specific with your messaging than being generic. I touched on this in the messaging part but to reiterate — the more specific your messaging, the more likely your ideal clients will recognize you are talking specifically to them, and they'll be less likely to walk past your copy to find their solution with someone else (who, chances are, is being more specific). Remember, being specific implies you're more of an expert (think specialist versus generalist) and for the most part, people would prefer to work with a specialist than a generalist.

2. Serving just your ideal clients will be more profitable than trying to serve everyone. One of the main benefits around serving only your ideal clients is you're working with folks who love you, love what you do, who YOU love, and they typically end up becoming your raving fans and telling all their friends about you. When you work with people who are not your ideal clients, that's when you end up with people you dread talking to, who are difficult (if not impossible) to please, who you end up jumping through

tons of hoops to make happy…and they STILL aren't happy, and after ALL of that, they may even end up asking for a refund.

It's that whole 80-20 rule — 20% of your clients cause 80% of your work. And typically the 20% who are causing 80% of your work are not your ideal clients.

Now, of course if you're experiencing a slow time in your biz and a non-ideal client shows up on your doorstep, you may decide you're okay with it — but overall your business will be more profitable if you don't have the extra work, time and energy drag that comes from working with people who just aren't a good fit. (And you'll actually be doing everyone a favor by releasing them and allowing them to find the person they're meant to work with. Wouldn't you want your counterpart to release people who aren't their ideal clients but are YOUR ideal clients so they could come find you? Everyone would be happier and better served.)

3. In most cases, once you make a point of attracting your ideal clients into your business, you'll likely find there are more than enough of them to fill your business. You'd have to serve a super tiny ideal client group for that not to be the case (and I haven't seen anyone serve a group quite that small).

Now, if for some reason you do find you're in the minority and your ideal client group is too small, here's what I would suggest: first off, don't beat yourself up. The fact that you now KNOW is a good thing — you wouldn't have known if you hadn't tried it. So the next thing is to either switch to a different ideal client group (chances are you have a few different types of folks you enjoy working with) or simply add to or expand the current ideal client group.

Testing and tweaking is a part of marketing, and no matter how big you get, you're still going to run into a product not selling well or a marketing campaign not doing as well as you thought — this is just what happens when you're an entrepreneur.

So now that you know why building your marketing around your ideal clients is so important, are you ready to figure out who your ideal client is?

Great!

EXERCISE

To start, I want you to close your eyes and think about your favorite client. It doesn't have to be someone who even paid you; it could someone you helped for free.

Once you have him/her in your head, get out a pen and paper and start describing him. Be as specific as possible. What is it about him that made him your favorite client to work with?

What did you really appreciate about him? What did he appreciate about you?

Don't rush this process — take all the time you need to really get a good sense of who your ideal client really is.

Once you have a strong sense of who your ideal clients are, not only will you be in a position to write really powerful copy to attract them (more on that in later chapters) but you'll also have a much better idea of where to find them. Instead of wasting time and money on places where your ideal clients aren't hanging out (and worse, you don't even know they aren't there because you haven't done this work), you can instead focus on where your ideal clients actually are.

And it doesn't stop there — you'll also have a better idea of which products or services to sell them, how you need to set up your business to better serve them, etc. That's why knowing who your ideal clients are is so important to all aspects of your business.

So what happens if, as you complete this exercise, you realize you have multiple ideal clients? As my earlier example around the stay-at-home moms showed, you really need different copy pieces to speak to each specific ideal client group. So even though technically you can have as many as you want, since it is a lot of work to set up different pages for each ideal client group, I would suggest you pick one and go (or "pick a horse and ride it" as the saying goes). You can always add a second one later if you're so inclined.

Now, we're going to keep returning to ideal clients throughout the rest of the book, so if you haven't done the exercise, I would encourage you to take 10 minutes right now and do so before moving to the next chapter. You'll get far more out of the rest of the book if you can start thinking about the

principles I talk about with your specific ideal clients in mind.

Chapter 4
PAIN VERSUS PLEASURE

Now that you know who your ideal clients are, the next step is to start connecting with them. And the first step in that process is to identify their pain.

If you're like so many of the conscious, heart-centered entrepreneurs out there, the thought of talking about your ideal clients' pain makes you want to run for the hills. You're trying to ALLEVIATE pain — the last thing you want is for your copy and marketing to be about the very thing you want to heal.

Okay, so first off, I get it. Yes, talking about other people's pain (much less mucking around in it so you make people feel worse) is uncomfortable at best and truly awful at worse.

But, let's talk about it - because there are a few things you may not have considered:

1. There IS a difference between pain and suffering. Pain is real — there is a problem in people's lives and they experience pain around it. In fact, I would even take it a step further to say that pain is NECESSARY. There are people who are born who can't feel physical pain and they tend to not live long. Their body can't tell them when something is wrong so they can fix it.

We need pain to keep us healthy physically, and we need pain to help us grow emotionally and spiritually.

But suffering is another story. Suffering typically happens in our heads — we magnify the pain with fear, shame, guilt or something else, and we suffer.

Pain is a part of life. Suffering doesn't have to be.

It's one thing to remind people of their pain so they can decide if they're either ready to find a solution for the pain or if they're not ready to move forward quite yet. If they're done with the pain, they may be ready for your product or service. If not, they're probably not ideal clients yet.

As part of the love-based copywriting approach, reminding folks of their pain is an important part of the process (which I get into more below). Twisting the knife so you cause suffering is not (and a lot of traditional direct response copywriting has roots in twisting the knife as much as possible, which is one of the reasons why it feels so yucky). It's a fine line, but a crucial one, and I'll talk more about how to walk that fine line.

2. Pain adds urgency. You would never call your dentist in the middle of the night and say "Oh my God, I missed my teeth cleaning, can you get me in now?" But if you broke a tooth? Or a jaw? Yeah, you'd likely be willing to wake your dentist (or doctor) up. This is why the following saying exists: "We're more likely to move away from pain than

we are toward pleasure." Remember, one of the main purposes of pain is to act as your alarm system to let you know when something is wrong so you can fix it. That's why when we feel pain, one of our first responses is to try and figure out what's causing it. Moving toward pleasure doesn't have that same power — sure, we'd love to experience more pleasure, but that urgency to make sure there isn't something seriously wrong isn't there. (This is why trying to sell without respectfully discussing your ideal client's pain is difficult.)

If you don't remind your ideal clients about their pain, they may say things like "Oh what you do sounds great; I'll definitely have to work with you one day." And of course, they never do.

But that doesn't mean the pain goes away. On the contrary, you may actually end up causing suffering, because your ideal clients don't know that working with you will actually alleviate their pain.

Look, people stand in their own way all the time. And unless you actually remind them they truly are IN pain while they're reading about your offering, they will be far more likely to brush it under the rug:"Oh, it's fine — I can deal with it for another few months until the kids are in school/out of school/ after the holidays/etc." Only by reminding them will you give them the gift of being able to choose — do they really want to stay there? Or are they ready to move forward?

3. People are busy. If you aren't clear about reiterating WHAT their pain is (so they know you "get" their pain) and WHY your product or service will solve that pain, they'll probably walk right by you, still searching for the person who can solve their pain.

4. Remember, the copy on your websites and sales letters (and really anywhere else) is part of a 2-way conversation taking place in your ideal client's head. So, you need to start the conversation where your ideal clients are — and where they typically are is in their pain. They know what their problem is and they're looking for a solution. Now, most of the time they have no idea what the solution is, so if you skip the pain and start with your offerings, again they won't have any idea that what you sell will actually take care of their problem, so they won't "get" that you're talking to them. Their pain, on the other hand, they ARE familiar with. So you want to start with their pain so you are actually starting at the beginning of the conversation (if you start anywhere else, your ideal client may feel like she walked into the middle of a conversation). Plus, this is how she'll also know she's in exactly the right place.

5. Because I know talking about pain can trigger negative feelings for some entrepreneurs, I would love for you to shift your perspective a bit. Ask yourself this: "What's keeping my ideal clients up at night?" Once you identify that, you can clearly see how your solution will help them sleep better. And if you convey that, you're definitely

headed in the right direction – the direction of love-based copywriting.

Honestly, it's really a disservice NOT to mention your ideal client's pain. Think of it as tough love — parents know they sometimes have to touch on their children's pain points in order to help them learn and grown. You're doing the same. Life isn't about feeling good all the time and if we deny the pain, we're adding to the problem, not solving it.

I'm also a big believer that the sales process should mirror the transformation your ideal clients will get working with you. And if you are a transformative teacher or coach, you already know there's going to be some pain when folks transform. If you don't give them the gift of going through their pain in your marketing or selling process, they may decide in the middle of working with you they're not ready to move forward — and that's when people disappear, drop out or even ask for refunds (and none of us want those things to happen).

At the end of the day, what you need to keep in mind is this — it's a disservice to not mention your ideal client's pain and it's also a disservice if you aren't respectful of their pain when you mention it.

Okay, so now that you're (hopefully) on board with acknowledging the pain, let's talk more about logistics.

First off, while I want you to talk about what's keeping your ideal clients up at night, I don't want you to wallow in it. My standard rule of thumb is around 30% (or even less) of any piece of copy should touch on pain — the other 70% should focus on pleasure/results/transformation/hope.

THAT'S love-based copywriting.

What people want to buy is transformation. Buying is fun (being sold to is not) and they want to buy the transformation. If you keep flogging the pain, that's not fun and they'll eventually stop reading and click away.

Typically it works well to start with the pain — remember, you want to start the conversation where they're at. And when you write about it, just describe it as objectively as possible. What are they dealing with every day? What's going on in their heads?

Where it turns into suffering is when you go overboard and start describing worst case scenarios or the "blood in the streets." One example where you often see this is in copy promoting financial advice — "The whole world is going to crash and burn and only I know what to do so you don't lose everything and end up in the streets with the rest of the rabble fighting over crusts of bread!" This is a great example of what I would consider the wrong way to use pain, which is more like "future spinning" — not just describing how pain is showing up in their lives right now, but taking it a few steps further to describe the worst, most dreadful outcome.

The way I like to do it is to use 3-5 bullets describing a few scenarios that are keeping my ideal prospects up at night, and then I start moving to the solution/transformation. I'll probably go back to some pain points later in the copy — just as a reminder of what they're going to be stuck in if they choose not to do something to solve their problem. (In other words, it also creates a sense of urgency — so people feel compelled to move forward NOW rather than waiting for the "perfect" time.)

Here's an example of what I'm talking about, from my Why Isn't My Website Making Me Any Money? sales letter:

> In fact, maybe some of the following sounds familiar to you, too:
>
> 💜 You've spent thousands of dollars or hundreds of hours (or both) putting up a website only to find it doesn't do much of anything for you. You feel stuck and frustrated because not only are you not reaching the people you're meant to help, but also, the money is gone and you're not getting a return on your investment.

💜 You have a genuine passion for helping people, and you know your products and programs will provide solutions that will improve lives. But something about your website just isn't clicking, because none of your prospects are buying! Making a big impact is trickier than you'd expected, and you're feeling discouraged.

💜 You know you should be doing something to make your website and marketing efforts pay off, but you aren't sure what that is. You've done tons of reading, and all the gurus and experts give different, conflicting advice. You've become "paralyzed" in overwhelm, so you don't do anything.

💜 You've tried a bunch of different marketing tactics already —emails, newsletter, giveaways, social networking... everything you thought you were "supposed to" do—but nothing seems to be working to increase your profits.

💜 To make matters worse, no one can really tell you WHY your website isn't effective! You feel like you're spinning your wheels, instead of supporting others the way you so badly want to.

See how those bullets talk about the pain without causing suffering?

Lastly, let's talk about HOW to identify your ideal client's pain.

EXERCISE

First, if you haven't figured out who your ideal client is, now is an excellent time to complete the ideal client exercise. If you have done it, take a moment to review your notes and "see" your ideal client clearly in your head.

Now, get a pen and paper and start answering the "What is keeping my ideal clients up at night?" question. Start writing everything they might be thinking. Don't hold back, don't try and censor and, above all, don't put it into "marketing speak." What are the actual words they would be saying? That's what you want to get to the heart of — not a summary of what their pain is but how they would describe their pain themselves, if they were talking to a friend.

THOSE are the words you want to use in your marketing copy.

You can also ask your current ideal clients what was keeping them up at night and why they decided to hire you. Write down EXACTLY what they say — their words and their phrasing. You want to mirror how they're thinking as closely as possible so they immediately recognize they're in the right place when they read your marketing copy.

Now, for some of you, this may be easier because the pain you solve is a more "urgent" pain — for instance, you help people make more money. But even if you offer something that is less urgent — like you sell toys for instance — there is still something that keeps your ideal clients up at night.

I worked with a client once who sold kits that allowed grandparents to write a book with their grandchildren. On the surface, it doesn't seem like there would be much that would keep the grandparents up at night. But if you dig a little deeper, there is definitely something — these kits provide a wonderful way to create lasting memories with their grandchildren. Grandparents can spend precious time with their grandchildren. And it allows them to share their own stories about growing up so they aren't lost.

Grandparents who long to create a deep, lasting connecting with their grandchildren and have a way to share their experiences and knowledge with their grandchildren are her ideal clients. And the pain of course is feeling like they're missing that connection and running out of time to share their stories.

You see how that works?

So even if it isn't immediately obvious, I would love to challenge you to sit with this exercise and really think about it. Once you scratch beneath the surface, you may be amazed by what comes out.

Chapter 5

WHAT IS YOUR "COME FROM" WHEN YOU MARKET?

One of the biggest keys to love-based copywriting is to take a hard look at both your mindset and "come from." Nail this and the rest of love-based copywriting starts falling right into place.

So what exactly do I mean by this?

Let's start with your "come from."

"Come from" refers to how you are approaching the copy you're writing (or have written). Are you coming from a place that's in line with the principles I've talked about in this book? From a place of abundance, love and wanting to attract your perfect, ideal client and trusting that this will work out to everyone's highest good? Or are you coming from a place where you want to make money "above all else"?

Now, before we go any further, I want to say a few words about making money — starting with I WANT you to make money. Look, the whole definition of being in business is to make money (otherwise you've either started a nonprofit association or you have a hobby), so you most definitely should be profitable and making money. Period.

In addition, if you're someone who wants to do more "good" in the world (i.e. give money away to worthy causes or perhaps even start your own nonprofit association) the more money you make, the more good you can do. So, if you look at it that way, not having a successful business that takes care of your financial needs and that provides you with the means to help others, if you so choose, is a disservice.

And my personal take is it makes good business sense to embrace the love-based copywriting principles in order to increase your profits. As I talked about earlier, love-based copywriting means you're attracting your perfect, ideal clients, who will rave about you, be easy for you to work with and won't be asking for refunds. And all that means your business will be far more profitable and less exhausting than a business filled with less-than-ideal clients. You also are more likely to build a solid, respectful brand (which can go a long way to help convince new ideal clients to give your products and services a try). And let's not forget, if you're someone who has a bigger mission — i.e. you want to transform the world or at the very least leave it in a better state than you found it, you probably resonate with building a biz based on love versus fear. I'm of the belief that you can't have a love-based business unless every part of your business is love-based (if even 10% of your marketing is based in fear, the whole thing is tainted with fear). So if you're not bringing your ideal clients into your business with love, you can't possibly have a love-based business.

BUT that means you must be willing to be fine with whatever happens during a promotion — even if that means you have less ideal clients who raise their hands to work with you than you wanted, not to mention being willing to let the less-than-ideal clients go even if they're willing to hand over their cash.

And that's what I mean by "making money above all else" — it's not a judgment around making money. It's a fact — you're willing to compromise everything including your time, energy, and maybe even some "long-term" profit in order to make more money now.

Now, I totally get this can feel really scary. Especially if your business isn't doing so hot right now.

The problem is, you can't "come from" a place of wanting to only attract, inspire and invite your ideal prospects to become your ideal clients if your mindset is one of fear, anxiety and worry about paying your bills. If you're worried about making money, no matter how good your intentions may be, it will be extremely difficult to be okay with letting less-than-ideal clients go.

And if you can't let them go, you'll be more likely to fall into using guilt, shame, fear, arm-twisting, or any other fear-based tactic that will work, just so you can "close the sale."

(It's a vicious cycle, isn't it?)

So what are your options?

To start, if your business is making money right now, it will be much easier for you to embrace the love-based copywriting mindset, so let's start with that.

Before you sit down to create a marketing campaign, close your eyes, take a few deep breaths, and really feel into the space of attracting, inspiring and inviting your ideal clients to join you. Feel them out there. Feel what they're looking for from you.

Once you can really feel into that, open your eyes and start writing TO them. BUT I want you to write to only ONE ideal client.

Not a group of them. Only one specific person. (In fact, I want you to go as far as seeing a name and person in your mind.)

And I want you to write to this one, single, specific ideal client as you would to a friend.

You know your friend is in pain. And you know you have the solution to get her out of pain. So wouldn't you be passionate about describing how your solution will help her because you just KNOW how much her life will transform?

Now clearly, you can't use this letter to your friend verbatim in your copy. What I want you to do is take that energy - that love-based wording - and put it in direct response copywriting format. Consider the letter to your friend a first draft; then go back and revise it. (If you'd like a step-by-step system to help you turn that passion into a copywriting format that attracts, inspires and invites, you may want to consider getting my "Love-Based Copywriting System" book — learn more at LoveBasedCopyBooks.com.)

Now, if the first part of this exercise sounds sort of woo-woo to you and you don't think you're feeling anything, that's okay too. A big part of this exercise is to get YOU into the space of welcoming your perfect, ideal clients. Because when you do that, you'll naturally start to reject phrases and word choices that don't feel in alignment with attracting, inviting and inspiring your ideal prospects to become ideal clients.

You'll be okay with letting less-than-ideal clients go, and by letting them go, you're opening the space for the perfect ones to walk on through. (Plus, you'll probably also start to naturally choose language that more specifically attracts your ideal clients.)

So now let's look at what you can do if you really need to attract money right now.

First off, there's nothing wrong with that. We've all been there. There is nothing to be ashamed of if you need your business to generate more cash.

The first thing you need to do is put together a focused plan. What is your plan to make the money? Are you planning on launching a new product or program? Are you going to be attending an event to attract new clients?

Now, I want you to make a conscious decision. Do you want to embrace love-based copywriting principles? Or are you willing to do "whatever it takes" to make the money?

There is no right or wrong choice here — but I want you to make a conscious choice. What I don't want you to do is to fall into fear-based copywriting because you didn't make a conscious choice about what you wanted to do.

I also want you to think about this — what happens if your plan doesn't work? What is your Plan B? (Big note here — as I already discussed, using fear-based copy MAY increase your initial sales…but it also may NOT. There are no guarantees here. So keep this in mind as you think through possibilities.)

Really take some time to consider this thoroughly so you can fully step into your choice.

Why am I being such a stickler about this? Because when you make choices subconsciously or you THINK you've made a choice to do something one way but you've subconsciously chosen a different path, things really get messed up. Disasters happen, the Universe brings out the 2x4, and suddenly you've made things a lot more difficult for yourself.

One clear sign you've fallen into fear-based tactics without consciously choosing to is if you find yourself making excuses — "Well, I can handle it," "It won't be so bad," "I know my program is really good and I'm sure it will help them even though it doesn't seem like they're my ideal client." If you hear yourself saying things like this, then you're probably making a subconscious choice – or you're about to.

What I would like to suggest you do instead is to not make an excuse but instead make a choice. You're choosing to do X — such as accept a less-than-ideal client and you're doing so because of X reason and you know it may be difficult but you're willing to accept the consequences because you feel like the consequences are less painful than not accepting this less-than-ideal client in the first place.

And when you make a decision from that energy, you are far less likely to end up with a disaster on your hands.

Now what if your conscious choice is to move beyond the fear and embrace love-based copywriting? What do you do to change your mindset from fear to love, and really feel that abundance and wealth will follow, even if you can't see it right now?

What helps here is any exercise that can help you expand, open up and feel abundant. So, for instance, exercises that tap into the law of attraction can work really well. I've also included a list below to get you started:

💙 Gratitude (making lists of what you feel grateful for and really feeling into being grateful)

💙 Meditation

💙 Journaling

💙 Affirmations — the actual definition of an affirmation, according to Webster's Dictionary, is "A statement asserting the existence or the truth of something." Basically, we say affirmations to ourselves every day, both positive and negative ("X always happens to me"). The practice of using affirmations to tap into the law of attraction is to purposefully craft a statement in present tense, that's positive, personal and specific. And once you craft it, say it to yourself over and over (say it out loud, in your head, write it down, etc.)

Below are some sample affirmations to get you started (and feel free to write your own; remember, being personal with your affirmations is important):

💙 I attract wealth and abundance easily and effortlessly.

💙 Wealth and abundance come easily to me.

- I attract my most perfect ideal clients easily and effortlessly.

- My business is filled with the most perfect ideal clients.

- Rituals to cleanse old energy that is no longer serving you and welcome in new energy.

- Grounding yourself — stand outside in your bare feet touching earth and relax. (Stand on the ground for at least 10 minutes. You may want to listen to music you enjoy as you do this.)

Also, depending on how stuck you feel, you may want to work with a coach or a program to bust through those mindset blocks. You can find resources on my blog — MichelePW.com/blog, including episodes of my PW Unplugged Radio where I interview top mindset coaches and experts.

Chapter 6

THE PHILOSOPHY BEHIND SELLING IN A LOVE-BASED WAY

Remember, buying is an emotional experience.

People love to buy, hate to be sold to, and absolutely abhor feeling manipulated.

And that, my friends, in a nutshell is why direct response copywriting has gotten such a bad rap.

Again, for years entrepreneurs used fear-based tactics to get people to buy, triggering feelings of fear, shame, guilt, anger and more. Now they did NOT do that because they necessarily enjoyed it, but because that was what was commonly taught. And the reason why it was taught was because it worked. And since a lot of copywriting teachers subscribed to the principle, "Why mess with something that works?," they kept teaching it.

In addition, a lot of marketers who are truly okay using fear typically fall into the "ends justify the means" camp. To them, all is fair in love and war, just as long as you join their program or buy their product.

And while there is no question there are folks out there selling crap, who are only in it to make as much money as fast as possible, I believe the vast majority of fear-based marketers truly feel their product or program will make a difference.

They're selling a quality product and they want as many people to benefit from it as possible — yes, because they'll make more money, but also because they truly want to help as many people as possible.

But, even though their hearts may be in the right place, I don't believe it works like that. You see, I don't believe the ends justify the means — I believe how you bring your ideal clients into your business sets the tone for your future relationship. If you bring them in with fear, fear will hover over your relationship. How will they fully trust you when they hit a rough patch? Would they be able to come to you openly and willingly for help? Will they give you the benefit of the doubt if your company doesn't measure up or makes a mistake? Or will they never quite trust you — viewing everything you do with skepticism — believing you're only trying to sell them *more*, as opposed to actually trying to help them solve their problem?

Remember, when you trigger fear in your prospects so they buy to get themselves out of fear, they really aren't dealing with the emotion. Instead they're running from it or burying it or numbing it, and now your company is all mixed up with that.

This is why, for many fear-based companies, they subscribe to the theory that if you don't have a 10% return rate, you're not selling enough. If you sell with fear, you're going to have a higher return rate, because the whole point of selling with fear is to sell as much as possible to as many as possible, regardless if you're attracting your ideal clients or not.

As the customer/client, if you don't really need the program but feel arm-twisted into buying, chances are very good you'll end up resenting not only the program itself (and the business), but the tactics used to get you to buy. And even if you actually enjoy the program, you may still have residual icky-feelings because of how you felt when you bought.

And that's why my belief is fear WILL cost you business. Sure, in the short term you may sell more than love-based companies, but between the returns and the slow erosion of your brand as your customers end up with bad tastes in their mouths because they didn't like the way they were sold to (even if they didn't fully understand it), over time I believe love-based businesses will be more profitable.

So, in order to become a love-based business, you need to sell and market by triggering love. Remember, since buying IS an emotional experience, the only way you're going to sell is to trigger emotions. Traditional direct response copy uses both love and fear — and, in fact, most fear-based marketers will actually use both love and fear (but, remember, if they trigger any fear at all, that becomes the predominant emotion). It's like the force in Star Wars — you can use it for love or you can use it for fear. It's your choice: which emotions do you want to trigger?

I'm guessing you want to trigger love-based emotions – that's why you're here!

Now, let's talk a little bit more about what motivates people to buy.

People only buy what they want. They do NOT buy what they need.

Yes, I'll say that again — they do NOT buy what they need, only what they want. If people only bought what they needed, they would have the bare minimum of everything — clothes, food, water, shelter and heat.

But we buy what we want because we don't want just the minimum that will keep us alive. If we did, we'd all be living in tents eating ramen noodles, wrapped in blankets. But we're not. We want clothes that reflect our style; we want the type of car we prefer to drive. We want our dream house, appliances to make our life easier, electronics for fun (and maybe to make our life and business easier), organic food for our bodies, and so on.

In other words, we want an upgrade from what we actually need. And that's what we buy — the upgrade.

However, since a lot of what we're buying IS an upgrade to a need, we can still justify the purchase by saying we "need" it. The reality is, we're still just buying what we want and justifying it by saying it's what we need.

So, where does "need" come from?

70

As I talked about earlier in the book, our needs often stem from deep emotional and psychological survival instincts (both for ourselves and for our species) that were implanted thousands of years ago when we were living as cavemen and cavewoman and wandering the world in hunter/gather communities.

According to psychology research, we haven't changed much emotionally since living in caves and running away from saber-toothed tigers, so many of our triggers have remained the same, such as:

- Security (having enough food, a comfortable house, warm clothes, etc.)

- Attracting a mate

- Raising a family

- Taking care of our health and our emotional and spiritual well-being

- Being a part of a community (including having a role in it – serving a purpose)

The reason why those needs exist is because they're essential for our own personal survival and for the survival of our species. Making sure those needs are fulfilled is deeply buried in our subconscious. That's why, if those needs are threatened in any way, we have an almost subconscious, survival instinct reaction to the threat.

That's why if there's a problem that's keeping us up at night, chances are it can be traced back to something that's threatening (or feels like it's threatening) one of those subconscious needs. And that's why we're "triggered," because we want to make sure we protect and fulfill our needs.

For instance — we're worried about money because that's threatening our deeply embedded desire for safety, for taking care of our family, and maybe even being a part of a community. It's not that we're worried about money per se — but what money represents — our ability to take care ourselves, our family, our community, our health, etc.

And there is no question the pain is real. Whether someone is truly losing his house or is worried he's going to lose his home even though it hasn't happened yet, the pain is real. It's there, it's real, and if our mission is to help people him keep his home, then we need to address that pain and that trigger, *so we can help him*.

So then the question becomes, are we going to use the trigger in a fear-based way, or a love-based way?

Triggers that are used in a fear-based manner tend to either twist the negative emotion that's already there, or create new negative emotions.

Triggers used in a love-based manner bring up the trigger/pain *without making it worse*. The idea is to create a buying environment where your ideal prospects firmly understand both the cost of staying in pain and the pleasure (transformation) that awaits them, so they can make a conscious choice between the two.

Now, I will be the first to admit this is a fine line, and a lot of what can make something fear-based versus love-based is the intention behind it (i.e. if you're truly committed to calling ONLY those who are ready to move forward right now, you're more likely to create copy that is love-based).

Remember, talking about the pain (and triggering the need) is simply the first step in the buying process. *Yes, you need to start with the pain or the problem, because that's where your ideal prospects are starting*. They're in real pain and are looking for a real solution.

Once they find a possible solution, they want to learn more about it — what the solution is, if it's real, if it will really help them, etc.

If their questions are answered to their satisfaction, they may take the next step and pay money for it.

So, if we go back to fear-based marketing and copy, in a lot of cases the pain is acknowledged via triggering fear-based emotions, because that will make the pain even worse.

BUT, in a lot of cases, there is then a "switch up" to love-based emotions, when describing the solution. Because what people WANT to buy is love, hope, transformation, community, respect, etc. Remember, buying is fun — if you keep going on and on about the pain, all you're going to do is turn them off.

This brings to mind a famous study where dentists were trying to figure out a way to compel kids to brush their teeth more. They divided the kids into three groups, and used three distinctly separate messages with each.

In the first group, they simply told the kids "You really should brush your teeth at least two times a day." In the second group, they said the same, but also included education about gum disease and other issues. It's important to note that they just talked about them; they didn't show any pictures. In the third group, they did all of the above, AND showed the most disgusting, horrifying pictures of what can happen when you don't brush your teeth.

So, which group do you think was the most likely to change their behavior?

Surprise - it was actually the second group. In the third group, the kids were initially horrified and said things like "Oh yes, I'm definitely going to brush my teeth more," but after a few days, their brains "buried" the horrifying images and their behavior went back to what it was before.

So what does this prove? When you go on and on about the pain, and turn it into suffering, along with dealing with all the other issues that fear-based marketing brings, you also run the risk of having your ideal clients simply "tune out" your marketing.

This is why both love and fear exist in direct response copy, because fear-based marketers used both. There really is no choice in using one without the other. Because people aren't going to buy if you only use fear. You need love in there, or it simply doesn't work.

This is also how fear-based marketers tainted love-based emotions. Again, when you mix love and fear, everything is tainted with fear. Even if you try and trigger love-based emotions with a fear-based mindset, it's going to sound more like fear.

Consider what's happened with hope.

Hope is a beautiful, love-based emotion. And yet, when I spoke to two of my colleagues who I very much respect, they both placed hope into fear-based marketing.

At first I was taken aback. Hope is love, not fear. But, then I thought about it, and I realized what was happening.

Just like when you approach pain via fear, it turns into suffering, when you approach hope via fear, it turns into false hope.

False hope typically happens when you sell a transformation that is unlikely to occur for the vast majority of folks. For instance, when someone sells the "You can make an additional $10,000 a month working an extra hour a week" concept, they're selling false hope. While yes, I'm sure you can find people out there who have been able to do that, it's not the norm and it most definitely isn't something you'll be able to package and sell.

At its worst, false hope preys on people's dreams. When I was deep in the fiction writing world, I remember the dozens and dozens of businesses set up to help writers get published. Now while a lot of those were downright scams, a significant chunk had enough truth mixed in them to be an actual business - but the success stories were few and far between.

So, when you talk about hope, make sure you don't fall into giving false hope via exaggeration, by promising miraculous transformations for *everyone* (yes even if you've witnessed miraculous transformations). When you're selling via love, it's so important to come from a place of love and abundance (not desperation), knowing that everything will work out as it should… and that *everyone* is being served at the highest level.

Now, once the solution has been explained, it's time to make an offer. If you make an offer via fear, it's probably going to sound very pushy and hype-y and sales-y. This is when fear-based marketers will typically touch on shame and guilt, especially if they feel like they're losing you. Or, they may simply try and steamroll your objections and exhaust you into saying "yes."

If that's how you view the process of making an offer, it's no wonder you want nothing to do with sales and marketing.

If you'd like to make an offer the love-based way, I'd like you to change your perspective, and consider making an offer as the opportunity to be of service to the people you're meant to serve. (My friend Lisa Sasevich often says it's a disservice to not make an offer – and I totally agree.)

You see, your ideal clients are looking for you. (In fact, I dare say they *need* you.) They are truly in pain right now, and if you don't make them an offer, they're never going to get the transformation they're looking for.

And that is a true shame.

Think of all the people you're meant to help that simply won't be helped without you.

Now, you might be thinking "But then maybe I should give it away for free."

Well, maybe. But let's consider this first:

As humans, we're drawn to live in and be an active part of a community. And, to live happily in a community, we're also wired to want "even exchanges" of energy.

You scratch my back, I'll scratch yours.

Money is simply a way to exchange energy. You give someone money in exchange for something they've put their time and energy into creating for you — whether it's a new pair of shoes or a book or a steak dinner or coaching program.

If you try and stop that flow, i.e. give what you've created away for free, what you've done is actually create an imbalance. People have your creation without compensating you in return.

And, when that happens, in a lot of cases, the people you've given your creation to don't value it.

So, they won't use it.

If you want to test this, let a few people who have expressed interest in your program in for free and watch what they do. In the vast majority of cases, what they'll do is nothing — they won't participate or even go through the information.

So, if you truly want to make the biggest impact you truly can, not only do you want to make an offer, but you should get paid when people accept it.

Above all, love DOES sell. People WANT to buy the emotions that are associated with love. Our job as business owners and entrepreneurs is to make sure we are standing in love and abundance ourselves, so when we reach out, our "come from" IS that of love and abundance.

We don't run after them when they say "no."

We don't make them feel bad when they say "no."

We don't encourage them to buy if we know in our gut they aren't a good fit.

Instead, we create the perfect buying environment for our ideal clients that respects their space for making their own decisions - and asks them honestly if they're ready to be done with their pain and experience transformation, instead. And we honor the decision they make.

In the next chapter, I cover specifics of how this looks in copy.

Chapter 7

CHOOSE LOVE-BASED TRIGGERS VERSUS FEAR-BASED TRIGGERS

Now it's time for the fun part! Let's roll up our sleeves and take a look at specific examples of how love-based triggers and fear-based triggers show up in copy.

URGENCY AS A TRIGGER:

Urgency is important because without it, there's no reason for anyone to buy now. They'll wait to buy for a better time, to have more money, etc. And in the vast majority of cases, when folks wait to buy, what ends up happening is they never buy.

That's why including urgency in your copy is so important. And urgency, in and of itself, is not the problem. The problem is fear-based copywriting tactics have misused urgency, leaving a lot of entrepreneurs with a sour taste in their mouth.

How do they misuse it? By making it fake.

Fake urgency is clearly made up urgency — like you only have 10 digital products to sell. Or you're out and out lying about why you either have a deadline or a limit on the number of products to sell.

So, the way to use urgency correctly is to not use fake urgency. Have a real, true-life reason why you're closing down enrollment or raising the price. Maybe the program is starting. Or this is the one time of year you have a sale on your product. (Stores periodically have sales with ending dates.) Or you're offering your time and there is a limit as to how many spots you're going to open.

Following are more tips on using urgency in a love-based way:

- Make sure you have a solid reason for doing whatever it is you're doing (closing enrollment, taking a product off the market or raising the price) — and clearly communicate that reason to your ideal prospects.

Good reasons for doing the above:

- The program is about to start and you want to take care of the folks who are enrolled.

- You're discontinuing the product (or you're upgrading it or coming out with a new version or some variation of that).

- You have a limited number of spots available because of the amount of time each participant is getting.

- It's a new product and you're offering it at an introductory price

- You're offering early bird pricing.

- You're having a sale — birthday sale, end-of-year sale, clean-the-closet out sale, etc.

- You can also use bonuses — either adding new bonuses or taking away existing bonuses — to encourage people to buy now. But again, there should be a reason why bonuses are being added or removed — maybe the bonus has a deadline (you're offering a special call on X date) or you're doing a final push and offering a special bonus at the every end. Or you can add a bonus that provides time with you, which has a natural limiter of only a handful who can do it since your time is limited.

- You can also use payment plans ending, but this isn't as strong as some of the other ones.

(For more ideas on having a sale or a promotion, check out my "Holiday Marketing Secrets" eBook report, which has ideas for sales anytime of the year: LoveBasedCopyBooks.com.)

YOU CAN ALSO COMBINE PAIN AND URGENCY:

In other words, let your ideal prospects know what the cost is to not ending their pain now. What is it going to feel like when they still have the same problem 3 months, 6 months, 2 years from now? Is that what they really want their life to look like?

Again, don't be overdramatic or use shame or guilt or sound judgmental or tap into fear — it's a fair question to ask them if they fully understand the cost of not solving their pain, and you can explain the cost. It becomes fear-based when you go overboard.

The easiest way to do this in a love-based way is to simply restate the pain you touch on at the beginning. An example is below:

> Ask yourself this: Where will I be in three months time?
>
> Will you still be struggling with your marketing? Not getting the leads or clients you need to keep your business alive?

USING PLEASURE AS A TRIGGER:

In love-based copy, you want to focus on the transformation your ideal clients are looking for. People buy hope — so give them hope. Spend most of the copy on the transformation they'll receive and make it clear that YES, this transformation is open to them, as well. People just like them were able to transform — they can do it too. That's very compelling and inviting.

NOT USING EXAGGERATION AS A TRIGGER:

Okay, so this is about what not to do instead of what to do, but this is too important to not talk about.

Exaggerating and over-exaggerating is the lazy way to get people to take action — you exaggerate the pain or the fear AND you exaggerate the results or the transformation. However, when you exaggerate, you also trigger people's natural skepticism, so while you may get their initial attention, you may NOT get the desired action unless you take steps to overcome the skepticism (and no, just saying "it sounds incredible but it's true" doesn't work).

So keep it real. If you've truly tapped into what your ideal clients are looking for — what's keeping them up at night and what transformation they're looking for — there's no need to exaggerate.

"UNSELLING" AS A TRIGGER:

Unselling (or "take away" selling) is when you take the sale away. In other words, you can actually clarify who would not be right for the program. This can be a powerful way to make it clear to your ideal prospects the consequences of the choice they're making.

The way you normally see this, is something like:

> Who is right for the program? (Then, use bullets
> to describe who you're looking for.)
>
> Who is not right for the program? (Then, use
> bullets to describe who you're not looking for.)

When you see this done in a fear-based way, there tends to be a lot of shaming and making people feel "less than" because they don't measure up. If you approach this in a love-based way, you can simply clarify, without judgment, who you're looking for and let your ideal prospects sort out if they're ready to move forward with your solution or not.

Here's a fear-based example:

> Successful people make time for programs like
> this because they know it's going to change their
> life. If you don't feel like you can make the time,
> you're probably not ready to be successful yet.

Here's an example of how you can do this in a love-based way:

> This program is not for everyone. If you're more
> comfortable growing slowly and taking things
> one step at a time, this is not for you. And that's
> fine, not everyone wants to move quickly. But if
> you're someone who wants to go big fast and
> take a quantum leap in your business, then this
> may be exactly what you're looking for.

And lastly, if it doesn't feel good to you, don't use it. Look, it's your business and your reputation. If you don't like how something is phrased or the choice of words, then don't use it. Find another way to say it that feels good to you. (And if you're working with an independent copywriter, I encourage you to have a conversation with the copywriter. I know when I work with clients and see edits — I always look at the edits from the perspective of "Will this hurt conversions?" If I believe what the client wants to change won't make a difference in conversions, I'll leave the changes. But if I believe their changes will hurt conversions, I'll ask why they want to change it, and depending on their answer, I'll look for another way to accomplish the same goal.)

So, now that we've covered the basics of love-based copywriting, let's take a moment in the final chapter to pull it all together.

Chapter 8
PULLING IT ALL TOGETHER

Now that you understand the main principles of love-based copywriting, the last step is to help you implement these principles into your own marketing and copywriting.

As I've shared, my own feeling is there is a lot of good in direct response copywriting, and if we approach direct response copywriting from a love-based perspective, we'll be able to grow our business and make a bigger difference in the world, and feel great about how we do it.

I've shared the main ways fear can show up in copy and given you ways to replace fear with love. And if you combine that with a love-based mindset and "come from," and write to your ideal client as if you are writing to a friend, you should be well on your way to creating love-based copy.

(Want some additional help? I've put together a love-based copywriting template to make it even easier to integrate what you learned in this book into your own copy and marketing. You can download the template for free at: LoveBasedCopywritingBook.com/template.)

Depending on where you are now and where you want to go, I've also put together a collection of resources to help you on your love-based journey in the Resources section.

Lastly, remember we are stronger together than we are alone. If all of us start to implement love-based copywriting principles, we will transform the direct response copywriting industry. None of us can do it alone, but together we can have an impact.

And when that happens, imagine how wonderful it will be to know that our marketing is a force of good and love as strong as our gifts and missions are.

That's when we know we've truly made a difference!

Love and success,

Michele PW

Book 2

LOVE-BASED COPYWRITING SYSTEM:

A STEP-BY-STEP PROCESS TO MASTER WRITING COPY
THAT ATTRACTS, INSPIRES AND INVITES

by Michele PW (Michele Pariza Wacek)

Introduction —
WHY LOVE-BASED COPY?

When I wrote my first copywriting book, "Love-Based Copywriting Method: The Foundation for Writing Copy That Attracts, Inspires and Invites" (which you can check out on Amazon or LoveBasedCopyBooks.com), I wanted the book to be about the philosophy of love-based copy, rather than the nuts and bolts of writing copy.

(Copywriting is writing promotional materials for businesses. Nothing to do with putting a copyright on something or protecting your intellectual property. And direct response copywriting (or direct response copy), which is what both this book and my first copywriting book is all about, is about crafting promotional materials that inspire people to take action — click on a link, give you their name and email address, or buy a product from one of those long sales letters where you're scrolling down forever looking for the price.)

The reason I wrote the first "Love-Based Copywriting" book is because over the years, I've met countless entrepreneurs who were between a rock and a hard place. They wanted the benefits of direct response copy in their business: they wanted to leverage their time, energy and money, while marketing one-to-many and automating their sales and marketing to free up their time and allow them to reach more people than they could without it…

1

But they hated how it made them feel.

Inauthentic. Hype-y. Sales-y. Slime-y. Like a used car salesman.

So what were they to do? Pull up their big girl (or big boy) panties and use it even though they secretly hated it? Or not use it, and forgo all those fabulous benefits direct response copy brings to their business?

Well, now there's a third choice: use love-based copy instead.

You see, whether love-based or fear-based, both are a part of direct response copy, because direct response copy works by tapping into emotions. And you need to tap into emotions because buying (or really taking any type of action) is an emotional process — so without the emotions, people won't move forward.

But you have a choice. You can choose to sell via fear-based emotions (fear, shame, guilt, worry) or you can choose to sell via love-based emotions (hope — which is not to be confused with false hope — love, pleasure, compassion, connection).

Traditionally, most direct response copy tapped into fear — hence it feeling so bad. But tapping into fear in order to create direct response copy that still sells for you is not required. You CAN choose to sell - and market - with love.

And that's what my first book was about — explaining and delving into the love-based copy philosophy.

And it got a HUGE response — bigger than I expected. I had people emailing and messaging me how that book changed their life. I had people making my book a required resource for their students.

I knew what I was teaching was super-important and needed, but still, I was unprepared for the passionate response I received.

And that's when I knew I had to write this book.

Now, to be completely accurate, I had already decided I needed to write a more "nuts and bolts" copywriting book, and that was going to be my second book. But with the response from the first book, I realized I needed to combine taking the love-based copy approach deeper, while teaching more of the foundational copywriting pieces.

And that's what I've aspired to do with this book.

So, this book is for you if:

- 💜 You're new to the world of direct response copywriting and want more step-by-step instruction on the fundamentals.

❤ You love the idea of love-based copy approach and want to learn more about how to take it deeper.

❤ You have a grasp of basic copy principles, but you're not happy with your results and are looking to sharpen your skills while getting better at writing love-based copy.

In other words, this book is for you if you want to go deeper and master the fundamentals. If that's you – and you're ready to learn the Love-Based Copywriting System — let's get started.

(And if you want to dig more deeply into the love-based copy philosophy, including exercises to help you write (and market/sell) in a more love-based way, my "Love-Based Copywriting Method: The Foundation for Writing Copy That Attracts, Inspires and Invites" may be perfect for you. You'll gain a better understanding of how to market and sell yourself with love, including a more in-depth look at the psychology of inspiring and inviting your prospects to take action using love-based triggers (plus how to avoid fear-based triggers). Go here to learn more: www.LoveBasedCopyBooks.com)

How to Best Use This Book

Let me start by giving you a little overview of what to expect and how best to use not only this book, but the entire system:

- Start by downloading the complimentary Love-Based Copywriting System Companion Workbook at www. lovebasedcopywritingbook.com/workbook. The book and workbook are designed to go together so you not only learn the Love-Based Copywriting System, but you can also start writing in a love-based way. The workbook contains even more exercises and writing prompts to help you craft your marketing materials.

The workbook is a pdf, so you can either print it out or just have it open in your computer's browser or tablet as you work through the book and exercises.

- It's also best (although not required) to have a project in mind as you go through the system. For instance, maybe you want to write (or rewrite) your website, or maybe you want to craft a sales letter.

If you have an actual, specific project in mind, it will help bring the lessons home so you can better incorporate what you learn into your copy.

If you don't, you can still get a lot out of reading this book, but there IS a difference between reading and doing. When you actually work through the exercises, you'll take the learning to a deeper level. And if you have a specific project in mind, that will help you stay motivated as you go through the exercises.

- ❤ The first 2 chapters are devoted to helping you set the stage before you dig into the actual writing itself. Those chapters provide you with background/ foundational information, and keep that dreaded affliction called "writer's block" from visiting.

- ❤ Next come the actual how-to chapters. Each chapter covers one foundational principle of direct response copywriting, such as headlines, features and benefits, objections, etc. I cover them "in order" — in other words, how they appear on a page (i.e. I start with headlines, then beginnings, then your story, etc.).

- ❤ Those chapters begin by teaching the principle itself, and include exercises so you practice what you learned – be sure to complete them as you go.

- ❤ You'll also see "Love-Based Tips" throughout, which give you even more suggestions for making your copy even more love-based. (Even though I teach in a love-based way, the tips are there to help you be more conscious about the choices you're making, so you truly are writing love-based copy.)

- ❤ Lastly, there are two "what's next" chapters — the first is about applying the Love-Based Copywriting

System to emails, website copy, sales letters, opt-in pages and even snail mail direct response letters, so you'll be covered no matter what your current copy needs – and the second covers advanced tactics and tips.

While there is no right way or wrong way to go through the system, my suggestion is to keep it simple. Start by reading the chapter, and by completing the corresponding exercises in the workbook. Again, if at all possible, use the project you're currently working on as the basis for the exercises. That way, once you've completed the system, you'll also have a first draft of your marketing materials as well!

Are you excited to start attracting, inspiring and inviting your ideal clients to do business with you? I know I am! Let's jump right in!

Part 1

WHAT TO DO BEFORE
THE WRITING STARTS

Chapter 1
YOUR PRE-WRITING CHECKLIST

Regardless of whether you're a professional writer or someone who dreads facing the blank page, rarely does anyone simply sit down and pop out a beautifully crafted piece of prose, "just like that."

They sweat. They struggle. They feel like everything they're producing is crap. And yes, even professional writers suffer from writer's block.

Now, one tip most professional writers have mastered to combat things like writer's block is to make sure they're fully prepared before they sit down to write (trust me, a lack of preparation is an invitation for writer's block to show up!).

So to make sure YOU'RE prepared before you sit down to write one word, here's a checklist of what to do before the writing starts.

- **Do your homework.** Research is an important part of writing, so before you sit down to write, make sure you have a solid understanding of your subject matter. That may mean making sure your notes are complete or creating an outline to identify where the holes are, or doing some online research.

I would also suggest you review all your notes and written materials the day before you're planning to start writing — don't write — just review. Then let your subconscious work on it while you sleep. You'll be amazed at how easily everything flows after this!

✓ **Know your ideal clients.** I'm a big believer in ideal clients versus target markets or niche markets, as I don't feel like niche markets/target markets are narrow enough.

You see, niche/target market tends to be more demographically-based and describe external factors. For example: stay-at-home moms, between the ages of 30 and 50, who are looking for a home-based business opportunity.

Ideal clients, on the other hand, are defined by internal factors — values, motivations, core beliefs. An example of an ideal client is a stay-at-home mom, between the ages of 30 and 50, who is looking for a business opportunity because she feels like she's losing her identity in her family. Her financial needs are met but her emotional needs are not, and she wants something more for herself.

See the difference?

So how do you figure out who your ideal client is?

EXERCISE

Close your eyes and think about your favorite client. It doesn't have to be someone who even paid you; it could someone you helped for free.

Once you have him/her in your head, get out a pen and paper and start describing him/her. Be as specific as possible. What is it about him that made him your favorite client to work with? What did you really appreciate about her? What did she appreciate about you?

(*Be sure to check out the companion workbook for more about your ideal client, as I've included more questions and prompts there. Also, if you want to delve into this even further, you may want to create an ideal client "avatar" to have in mind as you write your copy – I cover this in the workbook as well.)

Important: Don't rush this process — take all the time you need to really get a good sense of who your ideal client really is.

Once you have a strong sense of who your ideal client is, not only will you be in a position to write really powerful copy to attract him/her (more on that in later chapters), but you'll also have a much better idea of where to find him. Instead of wasting time and money on places where your ideal client isn't hanging out, you can instead focus on where he actually is.

And it doesn't stop there — you'll also have more of an idea what products or services to sell him, how you need to set up your business to better serve him, etc. That's why it's so important - to all aspects of your business - to know who your ideal client is.

So what happens if, as you complete the exercise, you realize you have multiple ideal clients? Alas, you really need different copy pieces to speak to each specific ideal client group — trying to combine them by mixing messages only makes you look like a "jack of all trades, master of none," and most folks want an expert to solve their problem. (After all, once someone has decided to finally get their problem solved, the last thing they want to do is screw around with less-than-ideal solutions that either might not work for them or might take a lot longer to work. That's why, in most cases, they'd much rather hire the expert/specialist from the start, and be done with it.)

So even though you can technically have as many ideal client groups as you want, since it is a lot of work to set up different pages for each ideal client group, I would suggest you pick one and go (or "pick a horse and ride it" as the saying goes). You can always add a second one later if you're so inclined.

✔ **Know your ideal client's pain (or what's keeping them up at night).** This is one of the most misunderstood parts of love-based copywriting. A lot of people, when I bring up the difference between fear-based and love-based copy, assume pain lies within fear.

But what they're confusing is the difference between pain and suffering.

You see, pain is real — there is a problem in people's lives and they have pain around it.

I would take it one step further and say that pain is a NECESSARY part of life. If you don't have pain in your body, how do you know something is wrong? If you don't experience pain in some way, how do you grow as a person?

For better or for worse, pain is a part of the life we live here on earth. (And maybe part of the reason pain exists is so that we know what pleasure feels like.)

But suffering is a whole other story.

Suffering typically happens in our head — we magnify the pain using fear, shame, guilt, worry, anxiety, etc. and we suffer.

Pain is a part of life. Suffering doesn't have to be.

It's one thing to remind people of their pain so they can make the decision if they're either ready to find a solution for the pain or if they're not ready to move on it quite yet. If they're done with the pain, they may be ready for your product or services. If not, they're probably not an ideal client yet.

As part of the love-based copywriting approach, reminding folks of their pain is an important part of the process. Making them feel worse so you cause suffering is not (and a lot of traditional direct response copywriting has roots in "agitating the pain" as much as possible, which is one of the reasons why it feels so yucky to do.) It's a fine line, and a crucial one.

In addition, pain adds urgency and, if done right, can help weed out people who truly aren't ready to transform (and who are therefore more likely to be unhappy, disappear from your program, tell others about their "bad" experience, and ask for a refund, because they're resisting doing what they need to be doing).

Now, in order to be able to talk about your ideal client's pain (or what's keeping her up at night) you need to know what that pain is. Here's an exercise to get you started:

(Note: If you haven't figured out who your ideal client is, now is an excellent time to complete the ideal client exercise in the workbook. If you have done it, take a moment to review your notes and "see" your ideal client clearly in your head.)

EXERCISE

Get a pen and paper and begin answering the "What is keeping my ideal client up at night?" question. Start writing everything she might be thinking. Don't hold back, don't try and censor and, above all, don't put it into "marketing speak." What are the actual words she would be saying, if she were speaking to you right now? That's what you want to get to the heart of — not a summary of what her pain is, but how she would describe the pain herself, if she were talking to a friend.

THOSE are the words you want to use in your marketing copy.

You can also reach out and ask your current ideal clients what was keeping them up at night before, and why they decided to hire you. Write down EXACTLY what they say — their words and their phrasing. You want to mirror how they're thinking as closely as possible so your ideal prospects immediately recognize they're in the right place when they read your marketing copy.

- **Start with the end in mind.** I'm actually a big believer in this, no matter what you're writing — including novels and blog posts — but especially for direct response copy, you want to be super-clear about the next step you want your ideal client to take.

Remember, direct response is called "direct response" because your ideal prospects are directly responding to the marketing material in front of them. So, if you want to inspire your ideal prospects to actually take action, you better know what action you want them to take.

Then, once you know what action you want your ideal prospects to take, you can craft the rest of the copy to support them taking it.

So, as part of the planning process, make sure you're very clear as to the action you want your ideal prospects to take after reading your copy.

✓ **Make sure your mindset and "come from" are in alignment.** This is another cornerstone of the love-based copy philosophy. Your "come from"(which is the place you're coming from when you write copy) and your mindset both should be from a place of abundance rather than scarcity. As much as possible, you need to be open to whatever happens (including maybe not getting the sales you want) versus being way too attached to individual sales.

When you're too attached to making a sale (especially if you're in a place of financial fear or anxiety), it's way too easy to fall into fear-based marketing and decide the ends justify the means.

So what do you do, if this is the case?

To start, if your business is making money right now, it will be much easier for you to embrace the love-based copywriting mindset, so let's start with that.

Before you sit down to create a marketing campaign, close your eyes, take a few deep breaths, and really feel into the space of attracting, inspiring and inviting your ideal prospects to join you. Feel them out there. Feel what they're looking for from you.

Once you can really feel into that, open your eyes and start writing TO them. BUT I want you to write to only ONE ideal client.

Not a group of them. Only one specific person. (In fact, I want you to go as far as seeing a name and image of the person in your mind.)

And I want you to write to this one, single, specific ideal client *as you would to a friend.*

You know your friend is in pain. And you know you have the solution to get her out of pain. So wouldn't you be passionate about describing how your solution will help her, because you just KNOW how much her life will transform?

**That's the energy you want to be in
when you write love-based copy.**

Now, if the first part of this exercise sounds sort of woo-woo to you and you don't think you're feeling anything, that's okay too. One of the points of this exercise is to get YOU into the space of welcoming your perfect, ideal clients. Because when you do that, you'll naturally start to reject phrases and word choices that don't feel in alignment with attracting, inviting and inspiring your ideal prospects to become ideal clients.

You'll be okay with letting less-than-ideal-clients go, and by letting them go, you're opening the space for the perfect ones to walk on through. (Plus, you'll probably also start to naturally choose language that more specifically attracts your ideal clients.)

So now let's look at what you can do if you really need to attract money right now.

First off, there's nothing wrong with that. We've all been there. There is nothing to be ashamed of if you need your business to generate more cash. (After all, one of the reasons why businesses even exist is to generate money.) But you need to make a conscious choice. Do you still want to embrace love-based copy principles? Or are you okay using whatever marketing and copywriting tactic that works (including fear-based) to make the sale?

There's no right or wrong here - only a conscious choice.

If your conscious choice is to move beyond the fear and embrace love-based copywriting, then *the first step is to change your mindset from fear to love.*

What helps here is any exercise that can help you expand, open up and feel abundant. So, for instance, exercises that tap into the law of attraction can work really well when it comes to changing a mindset.

Here are a few areas you can focus on to get started:

- Gratitude (make lists of what you feel grateful for and really feel into being grateful)

- Meditation

- Journaling

- Affirmations

- Rituals to cleanse old energy that is no longer serving you and welcome in new energy

- Grounding yourself — stand outside in your bare feet touching earth and relax. (Stand on the ground for at least 10 minutes — skin needs to be touching the earth. You may want to listen to some music you enjoy as you do this.)

(If you'd like to dig into the mindset and philosophy of love-based copy even deeper, then I'd love to point you toward the book that started it all — my first "Love-Based Copywriting" book. You can find more information about it right here: www. LoveBasedCopyBooks.com)

So now that I've covered the basics - what to do before you start to write, it's time to get writing! Next up – my best tips to help you get started, so you don't end up spending hours facing a blank page.

Chapter 2

FACING THE BLANK PAGE

One of the questions I'm always asked in my copywriting courses is "How do you actually get started? Especially if you're suffering from a bad case of writer's block?"

This is SO important, because even if you're not experiencing writer's block right now, it's bound to happen at some point. And since I don't want you to get stuck, following are some tips for setting yourself up for writing success. Now, these may not completely eliminate writer's block, but hopefully, they'll help minimize the times it rears its ugly head.

- The night before, make a point of reviewing all of your research including your ideal client, their pain points, etc. If you're comfortable with a bit of "woo-woo," you may want to ask your muse or subconscious to help out while you sleep, so you wake up inspired.

- Create a writing ritual. A lot of professional writers have a ritual around their writing time. For instance, I select and light a candle, then select and play music. (Plus I may also do some meditating and journaling before I begin.) Other writers will do something physical before they sit down to work, like dance or even walk around the block. (Check out the companion workbook for more ideas on creating a writing ritual.) It's really open to what you want to do. I would just encourage you to make it fun. Part of why it works is because rituals help prepare your mind to get ready for whatever you're doing — so as you go through the ritual, your mind knows you're going to sit down and write, so it can start to prepare itself. Then, when you finally sit down, the words start to flow.

(Love-based reminder — you could also do some of the mindset exercises from Chapter 1 to help you move into love and abundance, so you're in the right frame of mind when you're ready to actually write your copy.)

- Create an outline. I thought about putting this in the last chapter, and it could very well belong there too. For me, I like to use outlines as a way to prepare myself to start writing. By creating the outline, I'm getting my creative juices flowing so it's easier to actually write. Also, I create outlines at different times — sometimes I do it first thing (it's easier to create an outline than it is to start writing, so that can be my "warm up" to writing), sometimes I do it in the middle of the writing session if it inspires a brainstorm, and sometimes I do it at the end of a session to get prepared for the next day. If that works for you to be more creative in your use of outlines, go crazy. But if it's better for you to do it during your writing preparation time, then do it then. Either way, don't skip this step! It'll save you from losing your focus as you write, as well.

❤ Just start writing, even if it's nonsense. Sometimes people have a lot of trouble looking at a blank screen, so it helps to just *start* typing, even if you type "I don't know what to say" over and over. Eventually, your brain will kick in and you'll start writing. You can also end your writing session in the middle of a sentence or paragraph, deliberately, so you have an easy prompt to get you started the next day.

❤ Set a timer for 12 minutes and tell yourself you're going to write, no matter what, for the next 12 minutes … and then you're done for the day! Why 12 minutes? Well, apparently there's something that happens in our brain after we do something for 11 or 12 minutes, at which point, we'll suddenly find ourselves wanting to do it. For instance, exercise. Don't feel like exercising? Tell yourself you'll take a walk for 12 minutes and call it a day. Nine times out of 10, you'll discover you're actually okay exercising and you want to keep going. The one time you don't feel like continuing? Stop, just like you said you were going to. Worst-case scenario, you'll have 12 minutes of writing done on your project. Best-case scenario, you get yourself in the flow and you have a really productive writing session.

❤ Start wherever you want. There's no law that says you have to start at the beginning. I was talking to someone recently who told me how much trouble she had writing beginnings. She would stay stuck for days and days, just on the intro. I told her to start in the middle and work her way back to the beginning. It really doesn't matter what order you write it in, as long as it all "hangs together" before you send it out into the world. (And if this resonates, you're not alone. I've heard stories of novelists starting at the middle or the end of their books, and working backwards, so don't worry. This might work perfectly for you.)

💗 Finally, if worst comes to worst, leave and come back another time. There are always going to be days where nothing flows right and you're just really stuck. When that happens, the best thing you can do is step away. Go for a walk, call a friend, switch locations — maybe go get a coffee at a coffee shop, or take a bath. Or you may even want to just call it quits and dig in the next day. There's no shame in this — it happens to everyone. Just be patient and gentle with yourself. (But, a little warning as well — Resistance can rear its ugly head, too, so if you find you're getting stuck day after day after day, look deeper into what's really going on. An occasional "I just can't get my writing going" is normal — being stuck for days or weeks is a sign there 's something deeper going on. And definitely take a good hard look if this is a pattern for you every time you sit down to write.)

Hopefully, these tips will help you conquer the fear of the blank page. So now let's jump into actual copywriting tactics, starting with headlines.

Part 2

WHERE THE WRITING HAPPENS

Chapter 3
HEADLINES

Woot! Let's get started writing some copy!

So as I stated before, I'm going to be working my way down the page as you would see it (whether you're writing a sales page or web page) explaining each copywriting element as we go so that, along with getting an understanding of each individual element, you can also see how everything fits together.

And that's why we're starting at the very top of the page, with headlines.

Actually, to be more precise, it's a combination — prehead, headline and subhead.

Now, you don't have to have all three, but I do feel like the combination of them works really well together because each has a different "job."

Prehead: If there is a prehead, this will be the first text on the page (unless there's some sort of a banner with text on it — that doesn't count as text). It's typically a smaller font size than the headline below it, and it will sometimes be bolded or highlighted. And a lot of times (but not always) the wording will be something like:

> Attention Heart-Centered Entrepreneurs and
> Experts Who Would Love to Make Money
> Around Their Passion, but Don't Know How...

To me, this is the best way to use a prehead – a strong statement that calls out to your ideal client, so she knows you're speaking to her. Now, I've also seen preheads like the following: If You're Easily Offended, Don't Keep Reading." While that may be effective in some instances, I prefer preheads that clearly attract your ideal clients, instead of using it as a tease to just get people (ANY people – not just your ideal clients) to read.

Headline: The headline is typically the biggest font on the page, and a lot of time it's in a different color than anything else on the page. (In many cases, but not all, it's somewhere in the red family.)

While you don't necessarily need a prehead or a subhead, *you most definitely need a headline. It's the first thing people read, and 80% of the time, the headline is the "decision-maker" when it comes to whether or not your ideal prospect chooses to read the rest of the copy.*

That's why the headline is *so* important. Without a headline, without a *compelling* headline, your ideal prospects are going to walk right by your marketing materials and not even realize you're talking to them. (This is also why, when you're tweaking and testing your copy, the first thing you test is the headline.)

Headlines typically contain the big, bold promise of your offer. So for instance, a headline could be something like:

> Give Me 3 Days and I'll Show You How to Build a Successful, Profitable Business Doing What You Love.

In this case, the promise is to help other entrepreneurs make money doing what they love or are passionate about. So, if this is something that interests you, you probably will be intrigued enough to at least read on.

Subhead: Subheads are below the headline and in a smaller font (although not as small as the prehead) and a different color than the headline. (Blue is often chosen for subheads although you can really choose any color scheme you'd like. The goal is to make the headline stand out most, and the subhead second.)

The job of the subhead is typically to provide further details around the big, bold promise from the headline. So, a subhead that could go with the above headline might look like this:

> You don't need to sacrifice your income to do what you love. You CAN have both. Let me walk you through my simple, step-by-step plan to show you exactly how easy it can be.

So, if you put the 3 together, this is what you would get:

> Attention Heart-Centered Entrepreneurs and Experts Who Would Love to Make Money Around Their Passion, but Don't Know How...
>
> Give Me 3 Days and I'll Show You How to Build a Successful, Profitable Business Doing What You Love.
>
> You don't need to sacrifice your income to do what you love. You CAN have both. Let me walk you through my simple, step-by-step plan to show you exactly how easy it can be.

See how they all work together to build a story around who your ideal clients are, what's keeping them up at night (their pain), and how your solution can help them sleep better?

Okay, so now let's drill down into some more of the nuts and bolts of writing each element:

PREHEAD:

As I said earlier, to me the best way to use the prehead is to identify your ideal client. So, the best way to write a prehead is to go back to your ideal client exercise (see Chapter 1) and then craft a sentence that would appeal to who your ideal client is, while touching on his or her pain.

So it would look like this:

Attention IDEAL CLIENT who wants X TRANSFORMATION or doesn't want X PAIN.

Example:

> Attention Back Pain Suffers — Are You Ready to End Your Back Pain for Good?

Or if it makes sense, you can remove the actual "Attention" word — for instance:

> This Is for You If You're Ready to Live Your Life Without Back Pain…

OR:

> If You Suffer from Back Pain and Are Ready to Be Free from Pain, Read On. I'm Going to Show You My Simple, Drug-Free Solution to End Your Back Pain for Good.

(Note: The second sentence, "I'm Going to Show You My Simple, Drug-Free Solution to End Your Back Pain for Good" can technically be considered part of the prehead, or, you can use it as a headline.)

Depending on who your ideal client is, the "Attention" may not work as well. If your audience is someone with a clear title — like

Attention Speakers, Authors, Coaches and Experts — then the Attention works really well. Otherwise, you may want to play around with it, the way I did with the other 2 examples.

HEADLINE:

So how do you write a headline that attracts your ideal clients and inspires them to keep reading your marketing copy?

First off, keep in mind that IS *the point of the headline — to inspire your ideal clients to read the first sentence.* (And the first sentence should inspire your ideal clients to read the second sentence, and so on.)

So what would inspire them to start reading? Typically some form of curiosity, and one of the easiest ways to generate that curiosity is to talk about the solution to what's keeping them up at night.

For instance, if your gift is helping your ideal clients heal their back pain, your headline may read: "Finally — Live Your Life Free from Back Pain for Good." Your ideal clients have back pain — it's what has been keeping them up at night and they're looking for a solution.

Now, if you want to make that headline stronger, there are a few things you could do:

- 💜 You could add some sort of time frame — for instance "Imagine — Heal Yourself from Back Pain in 7 Days" or

"Give Me 7 Days and I'll Heal Your Back Pain." By adding a time frame, you've made it more specific, and the more specific you are, the more tangible and believable you sound. (Not to mention people like knowing exactly how long it's going to take to start seeing results when they buy.)

- You could add a guarantee (if you're comfortable with that): "Imagine — Heal Yourself from Back Pain in 7 Days...Guaranteed!"

- You could turn it into a story. "How an 80-Year-Old Overweight Man Who Suffered from Back Pain for 50 Years Finally Healed Himself for Good."

- You could answer a big "objection" your ideal clients may have, such as "Finally — Live Your Life Free from Back Pain for Good - Even If You've Tried Everything Else and Nothing Has Worked."

- You could make it a "how to" headline: "How to Heal Your Back Pain Without Drugs or Invasive Surgery" or "How to Heal Your Back Pain in Only 5 Minutes a Day."

- You could use the "if/then" model. It would look like this: "If You Can Watch a Video, You Can End Your Back Pain for Good." In other words, if you can do something pretty simple and basic, you can have the transformation you're looking for.

See how that works?

SUBHEADS:

The most effective use of subheads is to not only start "drilling down" into the details, but to also begin addressing objections.

So, for instance, with our back pain sufferers, perhaps one of their big objections is around using drugs or going through surgery to get rid of their pain. If you haven't already touched on how your solution doesn't require drugs or surgery in the headline, you could have it here instead, like so:

> YES, it IS possible to end your back pain forever without drugs or invasive, dangerous surgery! I'm going to teach you my simple, step-by-step system that will have you living and loving your life again, PAIN FREE.

Now, I actually covered a few objections along with drugs and surgery, which I'll explain now.

First off, I start with "It IS possible," because there are a lot of people who are skeptical about your solution (whatever it is). Chances are they have tried other solutions before, and they haven't been happy with the results. So, here's where you can start making the case around how your solution is different from what they've likely tried in the past, and how your solution will work, when others did not.

I also have the words "simple, step-by-step system" — if you DO have a simple, step-by-step system, this is the place to put it because people like to buy simple, step-by-step systems. They want something that isn't complicated, that they can easily follow, and that will give them the results they're looking for because they followed it.

I also end with the promise – the transformation — people who have back pain tend to not want to have back pain anymore, so repeating the transformation in the subhead is a good way to again connect with your ideal clients about what they want (so we're moving them more toward pleasure instead of away from pain).

While it is true people are more likely to move away from pain than toward pleasure (which is why respectfully bringing up pain is so important in your sales copy), by reminding people of the transformation they are seeking, you'll make them feel more optimistic and hopeful, rather than worse off than they were — because you harp on the pain.

EXERCISE

Remember, headlines are one of the most important elements of your marketing pages. Not only do 80% people decide to read the rest of the copy based on the headline itself, but the whole point of the prehead/headline/subhead combo is to encourage your ideal prospect to read the first sentence of the rest of the copy.

That said — don't stress out about writing headlines! Keep in mind that testing and tweaking headlines is a very common practice, and the only way to know if you're on track to crafting a hot headline is to actually put it out there and let the market react to it.

Also, keep in mind that spending time coming up with headlines is time very well spent. Even professional copywriters spend quite a bit of time on headlines. So, I would suggest carving out some time to play around with different headline options.

Okay, now let's dig into some headline-writing exercises:

- In order to know what's keeping your ideal clients up at night, you need to know who they are and what's troubling them. Exercises for discovering your ideal client and what's keeping him/her up at night are in Chapter 1. You may want to take a few minutes to complete them, if you haven't done so already.

- The best way to write a good headline is to write a lot of them. There are 2 exercises you can do — set a timer for 20 minutes and write as many as you can without stopping, or don't use a timer and write 100 headlines. (Now, each headline doesn't have to be completely different; you can change just a word or 2 and that still "counts" as a new headline.)

🐾 Typically the real headline gold happens right after you decide you don't have any other ideas for headlines (or maybe the 2nd or 3rd time that happens, which is why the 100 headlines is such a powerful exercise). Plus, as an added bonus, you may also end up with copy you can use for subheads, preheads or bullets.

🐾 If your headline ends up feeling long, don't worry. While it's certainly possible for your headline to end up being too long, typically, longer headlines test better than shorter ones. So, my advice is to start with a longer headline and test that. You can always test a shorter headline against it later.

The companion workbook goes into the headline exercise in more detail, if you'd like a little more support. (Remember, you can download it for free right here: www.LoveBasedCopywritingBook. com/workbook)

LOVE-BASED TIP: DON'T EXAGGERATE

Although exaggerations can come in all shapes and sizes, headlines seem to be more of an "exaggeration magnet." I suspect it's because you only have a few words to not only get a lot of points across, but to also get people to sit up and take notice.

But if you use phrases such as "I Would Have Walked on Broken Glass for This" or "Warning — Don't Bother Reading If You're Not

Willing to Change," you're probably raising people's BS antennas. And once those antennas are up, well, even if you're not intending on using fear-based marketing or copy, they're going to assume you are.

My suggestion is to instead *use strong verbs and nouns* that paint a picture without going overboard into exaggeration. (And if you're not sure if you're exaggerating or not, you probably are. You'll feel it in your gut if you've gone too far, so just listen to it. And make sure you sort out whether you're just nervous about taking a strong stance, or exaggerating. There's a difference between having a strong, powerful headline you might not have fully owned or stepped into yet and feeling like your word choices may be a turnoff — if it feels like a turnoff, then it probably is. If you're just having problems owning your value, then it's not exaggerating.

Chapter 4
BEGINNINGS

So far, we've covered:

- Preheads

- Headlines

- Subheads

which are all designed to encourage your ideal client to read the first sentence.

(And the first sentence gets her to read the second sentence, and the second sentence is designed to get her to read the third sentence, etc.)

So how do you craft a strong beginning that supports what you started with the prehead/headline/subhead? By starting in the same place your ideal clients are right now.

Think of your sales copy as a conversation — your ideal clients are "answering" your copy in their head as they read. So, if you don't start in the same place they're in, right as they're reading it, then to them it's going to feel like they've walked into the middle of a conversation and they're missing something, which means they're also likely to get bored (or frustrated) quickly, and click away.

So, how do you know where your ideal clients are, right now? Ah, it's what's keeping them up at night — their pain.

Now when you start out touching on your ideal client's pain, it's important to be respectful. Again, you don't want to twist or agitate their pain and cause suffering; *you simply want to acknowledge that you get it — you understand their pain and you can help.*

One of the easiest ways to do this is to have a 3-5 bullet points that describe a scenario familiar to your ideal clients. Below is an example from my "Why Isn't My Website Making Me Any Money?" sales letter:

> In fact, maybe some of the following sounds familiar to you, too:
>
> • You've spent thousands of dollars or hundreds of hours (or both) putting up a website only to find it doesn't do much of anything for you. *You feel stuck and frustrated because not only are you not reaching the people you're meant to help, but also, the money is gone and you're not getting a return on your investment.*

• You have a genuine passion for helping people, and you know your products and programs will provide solutions that will improve lives. But something about your website just isn't clicking, because none of your prospects are buying! *Making a big impact is trickier than you'd expected, and you're feeling discouraged.*

• You know you should be doing something to make your website and marketing efforts pay off, but you aren't sure what that is. You've done tons of reading, and all the gurus and experts give different, conflicting advice. *You've become "paralyzed" in overwhelm, so you don't do anything.*

• You've tried a bunch of different marketing tactics already — emails, newsletter, giveaways, social networking … *everything you thought you were "supposed to" do — but nothing seems to be working to increase your profits.*

• To make matters worse, no one can really tell you WHY your website isn't effective! *You feel like you're spinning your wheels, instead of supporting others the way you so badly want to.*

Notice how the pain is touched upon and acknowledged, but it doesn't make you feel worse?

Once you've stated the pain, you move on. That's it. You don't dig in, agitate it and make it worse.

So, what does it look like when you agitate the pain? Here's an example of the first 2 paragraphs of an "agitation" sales letter:

> Day-after-day, month-after-month, it's the biggest complaint I get. And as the weeks go by, it's getting louder. More plaintive. More desperate. It's a problem that is growing at an alarming rate. And if you don't get to the crux of it, it can cost you thousands or tens of thousands of dollars.
>
> In fact, it can even cost you your business.

In this example, the copy is purposefully trying to agitate you. The problem is growing, and if you don't solve it, it can cost you thousands of dollars or even your business.

But there's nothing tangible in those 2 paragraphs. They aren't targeting people who have already lost thousands or who have lost their business. They're targeting people who are WORRYING about losing thousands or their business.

Those 2 paragraphs are feeding into that worry all entrepreneurs have at some point or another when they doubt themselves, or when things aren't going as planned. Most of the time, that worry is unfounded. But because that fear already exists, if you so choose to, you can latch onto to it, agitate it and turn it into suffering.

Now, if you go back to the sample from my own sales letter, *I described tangible pain points that my ideal clients are actually experiencing.* I'm not agitating their worries about losing money and/or their business (which I'm sure many of them have). Instead I'm just respectfully letting them know I understand what they're going through.

EXERCISE

First off, you'll need to know who your ideal client is and what's keeping him/her up at night before you complete the following exercise. If you go back to Chapter 1, you'll find exercises for both of those, so please be sure to complete them before going further, if you haven't already.

Once you've gotten a handle on both your ideal client and what's keeping her up at night, here's an exercise to help turn that into your beginning:

Write a story around her pain.

Imagine your ideal client stuck in her problem. Maybe it's health, business, or relationship-related. What's the specific problem? What does it look like for her? How do other people treat her? What is she dealing with every day? How is it holding her back in the rest of her life?

Be as descriptive as possible — really describe how this problem has impacted her entire life.

Once you've written all of that down, go back and select the 3-5 biggest, most universal experiences. Maybe she's arguing all the time with her partner or she can't sleep from anxiety or she's been turned down for a promotion. These experiences should be specific, distinct, and directly tied into what's keeping her up at night. (And don't forget to go back to the exercise in Chapter 1, *and make sure you use words and language your ideal clients would use.*)

Now, turn those universal experiences into 3-5 bullet points you can use in the beginning of your copy.

Ta-da! Your love-based bullets are just about written!

(If you'd like more support in writing the beginning of your copy, make sure you download the complimentary companion workbook here: www.LoveBasedCopywritingBook.com/workbook)

LOVE-BASED TIPS: WRITING A POWERFUL BEGINNING

I actually have 2 love-based tips here:

1. Much like headlines, exaggeration is a problem in the beginning of your copy too. Painting a picture that's too dark is a good way

to tip the overall feeling of your copy right into the realm of fear-based arm-twisting. So, I suggest being objective.

As much as you can, describe your ideal client's pain objectively. Pretend you're a reporter and you really don't want to make your interview subject feel any worse than he already does. How would you describe his pain without wallowing in it or sounding gossipy/tabloid-esque? Also, imagine your ideal client as he reads it. How do you anticipate his reactions as he reads? Is he feeling more and more upset or discouraged or frustrated as he goes? Or is he feeling a sense of comfort and relief?

If you can master the latter, you've created copy that connects with your ideal client without agitating his pain. That also means he likely IS comforted and relieved, and probably thinking "Yeah, that's exactly how I feel — can this person help me?" And THAT'S exactly where you want him to be.

2. This one bears repeating: As closely as possible, use the words your ideal clients use.

Your ideal clients will recognize their own words in what you say, and realize you ARE talking directly to them.

There's no need to "dress up" what they're saying with marketing-speak (which can mean anything from trying to summarize what they're saying or inserting your own language in there or watering it down to make it more generic — *remember, being generic around what's keeping them up at night does NOT work*). All you need to do is restate what they're already saying when they can't sleep at night, *and then let them know you have a solution.* But before you tell them all about it, you want to first explain why YOU'RE best-qualified to provide it to them.

You do that in your Million Dollar Story section – and that's up next!

(Not sure what words they would actually use? Ask them! Talk to your ideal clients and ask them to describe their pain in their words. Also, hanging out in social media groups and taking note of how they describe their pain works too. Jot down the language you hear them using, and review your beginning before you complete the exercise in the next chapter.)

Chapter 5

YOUR MILLION-DOLLAR STORY

So far we've covered:

- Preheads

- Headlines

- Subheads

- Beginnings

And now it's time for your story.

This section is where you introduce yourself to your ideal client (or, more accurately, your ideal prospect since if he's reading this sales page and you're introducing yourself to him, he probably isn't a client yet). Note: Even if your ideal prospects know who you are, you still want to take the time to tell your story — even if you're tired of telling your story, your ideal prospects aren't tired of hearing it).

I like to call this section Your Million-Dollar Story. And don't worry if you haven't made a million dollars with your story yet; the potential is there.

Now there are a few specific things you want to accomplish with your story — as my friend Lisa Sasevich, Queen of Sales Conversion, says, "You want to showcase your credibility and your vulnerability." Plus, you want to share your "Big Why."

Your credibility shines through when you position yourself as an expert. *Your ideal prospects need to believe you actually have the expertise and experience to solve what's keeping them up at night.*

But, if you position yourself as TOO much of an expert, they can feel intimidated … "There's no way this is going to work for me because I'm so far below them" — which is where sharing your vulnerability comes in. If you can share how you've been where they've been and walked in their shoes, they won't feel like you're untouchable. Instead, they'll see how you truly do "get" them.

And, since passion is contagious, you definitely want to share your passion — which is where talking about your "Big Why" comes in. In many cases, there's an important reason behind why you started your business. Maybe it's because you were stuck exactly where your ideal prospects are stuck, and you're absolutely passionate about getting them unstuck. Maybe you have a big dream or a big message to share with the world. Maybe your family is what's most important, so you designed your business to put your family first. Whatever your "why" is behind your business, *sharing it can create an instant connection with your ideal prospect.* (And never forget, your ideal prospect wants to do business with actual people, not just a company, and they want to do business with people they know, like and trust.)

So, let's talk about how you can actually craft your Million-Dollar Story.

First off, I like to start with your expertise, which typically sounds like your bio. This is a paragraph or 2 that highlights your professional accolades — your experience, degrees, awards, books, clients who are well-known in your industry and, of course, results your clients have gotten. I suggest keeping it short but powerful — this is your chance to brag!

Now, what do you do if you're new to your business? You can either pull some accolades from your "other" career, or if you really feel like you have no expertise to share, you can simply jump into your Big Why story.

Next you want to move to either your vulnerability or your Big Why - or both. (Many times your Big Why is also your vulnerability.) And the best way to showcase this is by telling an actual story.

There are 4 parts to this story —

- Introduction

- Conflict

- Climax

- Resolution

(And, yes, if you've ever studied fiction, these do mirror the structure of a fictional story.)

The introduction sets the stage. What were you doing before the problem/challenge happened? For instance, maybe you just gave birth and you couldn't lose the baby weight, and your weight increased from there. Or maybe you quit your job to start your business and things started going south. Chances are there's something that happened that caused the problem/challenge, so you want to start right before that catalyst.

The conflict is the challenge you faced. For instance, you could have been broke, overweight, had health or relationship problems.

Typically (but not always) it mirrors where your ideal clients currently are, themselves. If it does, it can be far more powerful because your ideal clients will see themselves in your story.

The climax is the breaking point — what caused you to finally change. A lot of times it could be where and when you actually hit rock bottom.

The resolution is what you did to turn it all around, which also should be what your business is selling. (And the next part of the copy will go into your solution in more detail, but for your story, you should summarize briefly.)

Okay so let's look at an example of how this would work for a business coach:

Introduction –

→ Quit corporate job and started lifelong dream as a coach.

Conflict –

→ Struggling as a coach, barely making $1000 a month. Couldn't pay bills and started to rack up credit card debt.

Climax –

→ Called father to ask for another loan. Father says, "Why don't you get a job?"

Resolution –

→ Got focused and in 9 months broke 6-figures.

Here's another example for a healer:

Introduction —

→ Went back to high-powered job after giving birth to second child.

Conflict —

→ Constantly exhausted and stressed. Never have enough hours in the day to balance family and work, much less for exercising or self-care. Suffered from constant headaches and back pain. Medical doctors offered no relief.

Climax —

→ Pain and exhaustion continued to get worse and worse until collapsing one day and having to take time off of work.

Resolution —

→ Found an alternative medicine program that completely healed her where medical doctors could not.

See how this works?

EXERCISE

The best way to do this section is to start writing. A lot. Just get your whole story out and then edit it down. (It's a lot easier to delete than it is to add.)

Take a few moments and fill in the details under each part, now:

Introduction:

Conflict:

Climax:

Resolution:

Don't censor yourself — at this point, just write as much as you can. And don't get too worried if you're putting the right information under the right section. Right now, what's important is getting all the details on paper.

Once you've completed it, put it away for a few days before editing it. Getting a fresh perspective is a great way to best determine what stays and goes.

When you are ready to edit, you want to delete the details that stray from your main objective – those that go off into other directions. As much as possible, simplify your story (much like the examples above) so it's clear and simple for your ideal clients to follow.

Now, if you're stuck, make sure you check out the Love-Based Copywriting Workbook (www.LoveBasedCopywritingBook.com/workbook) for writing prompts to help get your creative juices flowing.

LOVE-BASED TIP: DON'T BE AFRAID TO BE VULNERABLE

I know it may feel really scary to show your vulnerable side, but the truth is, many times your vulnerability is what will seal the deal — not your credibility.

Sure, people need to believe you're an expert in your field, but remember, if you're too much of an expert, people will feel like you can't "relate" to what they're going through. And if you can't relate, you can't help them.

Your vulnerability is what makes you relatable. It makes you human. People can see themselves in you. And that's what helps them believe that, if you're just like them and can do it, maybe they can do it too.

Chapter 6

YOUR SOLUTION: THE BIG PICTURE OVERVIEW

So far we've covered:

- Preheads

- Headlines

- Subheads

- Beginnings

- Your Million-Dollar Story

Next up is your solution – and all the details around it. (Which is the perfect transition since you likely ended your story by talking about how your solution transformed your life and how it also has the potential to transform your ideal client's life.)

If you recall, Chapter 4 was all about respectfully acknowledging what's keeping your ideal clients awake at night. So, it only makes sense to follow that up with how your solution will help them go back to sleep, and rest peacefully.

How do you do that? *You make it clear EXACTLY how your solution will take care of their pain.*

Sounds easy, right? Not to mention obvious.

Well…

You see, most entrepreneurs make one of two big mistakes here. Either they focus on describing the features of the program (i.e. "My program is 5 Q&A calls plus a 300-page workbook") or they focus on a very vague solution, such as "My program will help you make money because everyone wants to make more money."

Or, in a lot of cases, they make both of these mistakes — which turns their copy into a mushy mess.

I'll talk more about features and benefits later in this chapter, but for right now, I want to focus on the problem (the BIG problem) with being vague.

Let's say you're a business coach and you help entrepreneurs attract more clients. At first glance, it sounds like a good thing — pretty much all entrepreneurs want to attract more clients, right? So, if that's what you do, you should have lots of people who want to hire you. Plus, you can't go wrong tying what you do into making more money, right?

Well…

The problem is, not only does that sound pretty vague, but it also sounds like every other business coach out there. (Not to mention the fact that it makes you sound like a generalist, and the vast majority of time, people would rather hire a specialist to solve their problems than a generalist.)

Part of the reason it sounds vague is because there are actually a lot of solutions to that same problem – the "wanting more money" problem.

Pretty much everyone would like more money, right? So what's wrong with promising someone you'll help them get it?

Well because there's about a zillion solutions to the "wanting more money" problem, depending on what you're SPECIFICALLY concerned about.

For example, let's look at some different money-making scenarios:

- An entrepreneur lands more clients.

- An entrepreneur launches a product.

- An employee gets a promotion.

- An employee lands a different, higher paying job.

- A smart investment in real estate or stocks, etc. pays off.

- Selling things on eBay.

Now let's look at some different money-saving scenarios (because if you cut your expenses without losing any income, you'll have more money at the end of the day):

- An entrepreneur's overhead is too high so he cuts it back.

- An entrepreneur thinks his employees are stealing from him, so he focuses on figuring out who.

- An family learns how to make - and live on - a budget.

- A family learns how to renegotiate their mortgage so they pay less each month.

What all of these things have in common is they provide you with ways to have more money at the end of the day. But the way to go about tackling each one is vastly different, because each is solving a very different money problem.

And, I guarantee you that what's keeping your ideal clients up at night is the SPECIFIC problem — not some generic "Gee I wish I had more money." They're thinking things like "I need a new job/ need a higher paying job," "I need more clients," "Where is all the money going?" or something else more specific.

Now let's look at a different problem — losing weight. That seems pretty straight forward, right? Consider some of the nuances:

- You want to lose 5 pounds (or 10) because your 20-year high school reunion is next month.

- You've been overweight for years and have tried every diet on the planet, only to have the weight come roaring back every time you lose it (plus a few pounds to boot).

- You just had your third child and now the weight isn't coming off the way it did before, with your first two children.

- You just turned 50 and suddenly gained 10 pounds and aren't at all happy about it.

- You're not just overweight, but considered obese, and you may need to do something pretty radical to lose the weight because your health is now in jeopardy.

See how specific each one of their problems are? Sure they all fit into the "losing weight" category, but just because someone sees a losing weight message, it doesn't mean he or she is going to buy what is being offered.

So, for your solution — the problem you solve — what can you do to make it more specific — so it attracts YOUR ideal client and sounds specifically like YOU?

I would start by digging deep. Really get clear on who your ideal client is and what EXACTLY is keeping her up at night, so you can specifically address that in your solution.

To demonstrate this, let's go back to the business coach example. When the business coach digs deep, she discovers that her ideal client hates selling herself — just hates it. And what she's really good at is helping them own their value, so they stop hating selling themselves and instead become pretty good at it.

See how more specific and juicy that sounds? And how that really captures YOUR unique gifts (not to mention how it no longer sounds like every other business coach out there)?

Okay, so once you've dug into how you specifically solve what's keeping your ideal client up at night, chances are you have a statement or a paragraph that's a "big picture overview" of your solution. For our business coach, it may look something like this:

> A step-by-step system to help you transform your relationship with sales, so you stop hating — and (maybe) even start loving — the entire sales process!

Once you've done that, the next step is to get more specific and describe the details, and the easiest way to do that is through features and benefits, which is what we'll cover in the next chapter.

But for now, let's get your big picture overview nailed down. But real quick, before you get started …

EXERCISE

As I said earlier, digging deep is the first step toward figuring out what your ideal client really wants, so you can be sure your solution gives it to them.

So, to start, make sure you did the exercise in Chapter 4 – Beginnings. Remember, it's crucial that you really get into your ideal client's head and figure out the specific nuance of the problem (in her own words) that's really keeping her up at night.

There are a couple of ways to do this:

1. Research — go out and talk to your ideal prospects. Ask them exactly what's keeping them up at night and how they want you (specifically you) to help. Really take note of their language. If you end up talking to your former ideal clients, you may also want to ask them why they ended up choosing you over your competition (this would probably give you some really good messaging and language to use).

Along with actually talking to them, you can also check out social media and see how they express themselves on those platforms when they're venting about their problem.

And if you have an email list of your ideal clients, don't be afraid to send out a survey and ask them to actually tell you — in their own words — what's keeping them up at night and what exactly they are looking for from you to help them solve it.

(Note, the way to have your ideal clients tell you things in their own words is to ask open-ended questions. I know in a lot of ways giving people a selection of choices they can pick from is easier, but it's not nearly as informative as asking an open-ended question and letting them tell you what's in their mind.)

2. Do some journaling around this. Imagine your ideal client and then really dig into not only what her pain is, but how she wants you to help. That's what you want to focus on - that little bridge between what they want and how you can give it to them.

3. A combination of the above two (recommended).

Once you've figured out the bridge — how your solution can solve their very specific and unique pain — edit it down so it's about a paragraph or 2, BUT (here's the catch) don't lose their specific words and language.

If it has to be a little longer, then so be it, but as much as possible - keep your ideal client's actual words and phrasings - and keep it short and succinct.

An example of this bridge could be this (from Lisa Sasevich's Speak-to-Sell):

> If you resonate with my Invisible Close
> philosophy, then you'll love learning how to
> craft a Signature Talk that magically transforms
> interested prospects into invested clients on-
> the-spot, and leaves both you and them feeling
> good about it.

In this case, her ideal clients want to learn how to sell using a Signature Talk, but don't like a lot of traditional "sell from the stage" programs (either it doesn't work for them or they feel terrible doing it or both). See how specific it is? It's not just any "sell from the stage" program, but something that is a very specific problem for a specific group of people.

LOVE-BASED TIP: STICK WITH WHAT WORKS

As you work on coming up with your big picture overview, I suspect you'll find yourself wanting to use some sort of new vocabulary to sum up what your ideal client is going through.

I highly encourage you to resist this temptation.

Here, more than anywhere else, you're going to feel the need to distill everyone's experiences into some cute, clever, marketing-speak elevator pitch/slogan you can spit out at networking meetings…and if you succumb to this, you'll probably find yourself surrounded by folks who suddenly find themselves needing to go refill their drinks.

Part of being love-based is being simple — just say what you mean and mean what you say. Don't dress it up or make it cute and clever (and whatever you do, don't twist it and use it as a weapon against your ideal clients). Be clear, concise, open, and respectful … and everyone wins.

Chapter 7

YOUR SOLUTION: DRILLING DOWN INTO THE DETAILS

So far we've covered:

- Preheads

- Headlines

- Subheads

- Beginnings

- Your Million-Dollar Story

- Your Big Picture Solution

Next up is drilling down into the details of your Big Picture Solution — and you do that using feature-and-benefit bullets.

Features and benefits are basically the 2 ways to describe your offer. Features are more "external" — they tend to describe the physical attributes of your product, program or service (5 calls, transcripts, a workbook, a live event, etc.). You can also think of the features as describing the "service delivery."

While it's certainly important to know what the features are/ service delivery is (since it is pretty important for them to know if they need to say show up for a live event versus download an eBook), the features are not what people are buying.

They're buying a solution to their problem, the transformation, the "what's in it for them."

That's why you need to spend more time describing the benefits than the features.

Typically what I like to do with benefits is turn them into a list of bullets, with each bullet describing one specific benefit or "what's in it for them." Below is an example from my "Why Isn't My Website Making Me Any Money?" sales letter – the benefits are in bold - (which you can check out in full right here: www. MichelePW.com/10easysteps)

> Here's a sampling of what you'll learn when you order your copy of **Why Isn't My Website Making Me Money?**:
>
> • The **biggest mistake people make when building an online business** (you've got to understand this, or you risk losing what could add up to thousands of dollars!).

- **7 tips and techniques to tweak your existing website in order to make it persuasive and irresistible to your ideal prospects,** so they are excited to work with you and experience the transformation you provide.

- One simple strategy that will make the difference between your site being "just a website" and it becoming an **online life-changing, business-building machine!**

- **7 simple, 5-minute tweaks that add credibility to your site,** so people will be more comfortable handing over their credit card and other personal information.

- **4 powerful strategies to start building your list** with interested, ideal prospects who can't wait to work with you.

- **And more.**

See how specific all of those bullets are? Each one captures one specific benefit. (In other words, don't try and combine a bunch of benefits into one bullet.)

Along with one benefit per bullet, each bullet should be focused either on moving your ideal prospect toward pleasure, or away from pain.

Here's an example of moving your ideal client toward pleasure:

> 💜 An easy and effective way to transform yourself into an expert (so people will be more likely to buy from you).

And here's one for moving away of pain:

> 💜 A common, VERY costly mistake you've probably made (or are considering making), which leads to your website not making sales (and how to avoid it).

In a nutshell, the moving toward pleasure bullets paint the picture of where your ideal prospect wants to go (in the case of the example, toward becoming an expert).

Moving away from pain involves touching on what's keeping them up at night. In the example above, it's about making a mistake that could keep your ideal prospect from making sales with his website.

I generally like to have a ratio of 70% moving toward pleasure bullets and 30% moving away from pain bullets. People are buying the transformation — that's what they want. But, to keep people from getting in their own way and "waiting" for the transformation, you need to remind them what's keeping them up at night so they can make the decision if they're ready to be done with it and move on, or if they need to sit and stew in it a little more.

Now, there's also an advanced technique where you either amplify the emotion, or resolve it. Typically how this works is you add the amplification or resolution at the end of the bullet, either after a comma or in parentheses.

An example of amplifying:

> ♥ An easy and effective way to transform yourself into an expert (so people will be more likely to buy from you).

The (so people will be more likely to buy from you) is amplifying the pleasure — the transformation.

You can also amplify the pain — but just be careful when you do that so you don't turn it into suffering. (More on this in the Love-Based Tips section.)

An example of resolving the emotion is here:

> ♥ A common, VERY costly mistake you've probably made (or are considering making), which leads to your website not making sales (and how to avoid it).

The (and how to avoid it) is resolving the pain of making a costly mistake.

Now, I also wanted to point out what's going on with this bullet:

> 💜 7 simple, 5-minute tweaks that add credibility to your site, so people will be more comfortable handing over their credit card and other personal information.

Adding numbers is a great way to make bullets more tangible. In this case there's a specific number of tweaks (7) along with a specific amount of time (5 minutes), which makes this bullet feel more "real."

And lastly, you don't want to share too much. Keep the curiosity level high.

Compare:

> 💜 You'll learn how a daily gratitude practice will help you attract massive abundance. (And the best part? It only takes 10 minutes a day.)

Versus:

💜 You'll learn how a simple, daily practice can open you up to attracting massive abundance. (And the best part? It only takes 10 minutes a day.)

The first one actually spells out that it's a gratitude practice, which immediately lessens the curiosity. Plus, if someone reading it has heard about gratitude practice before, he or she may think to themselves "Oh, I already know about that. I don't need that." And at that point, they've found a reason NOT to buy.

The second one doesn't share what the actual practice is, which bumps up the mystery/curiosity factor. It also adds the word "simple." (Words like simple, step-by-step, effective, efficient and proven are all great choices to add to your bullets wherever possible, as they strengthen the message.)

Okay, so to recap, here are the steps to crafting powerful, love-based, benefit-driven bullets:

💜 The more specific the bullet, the better.

💜 One benefit per bullet — don't try and shove a bunch of benefits into one bullet; this will overwhelm the reader.

💜 Each bullet should either move your ideal prospects toward pleasure (the transformation they're looking for) or away from pain.

💜 About 70% of your bullets should move your ideal prospect toward pleasure - 30% should move him or her away from pain.

💜 To make your bullets more effective, either amplify the emotion (see the Love-Based Tip below) or resolve it.

💜 Use numbers to make the bullets even more tangible.

💜 Don't reveal all — keep the bullet shrouded in mystery, so the curiosity factor stays high.

EXERCISE

Writing bullets is actually a 2-step process. First, you need to figure out what your features and benefits are, and then you can turn the benefits into bullets.

The easiest way to do this is to begin by taking a piece of paper and drawing a line down the center, so you have 2 columns. Label one column "Features" and the other "Benefits."

Start by listing all the features — all the factual aspects of your product (think: deliverables) or, if it's an information product, what your product covers.

Then, turn each of those features into a benefit using the phrase "so that."

Example - information product:

You teach people how to lose weight. So one of your features may be:

Nutritional information.

You turn that into a benefit like this:

> I teach nutritional information so that you know what to eat and what to avoid so that you not only lose weight faster but keep it off longer so that you love what you see when you look in the mirror.

Note how I kept using the words "so that" to *keep drilling down in order to uncover even deeper benefits*, which gets us even closer to what your ideal prospects are REALLY looking for.

And, if you notice, I didn't stop at "losing weight." Losing weight is actually NOT the "end" game — people want to lose weight so they look better, feel better, live longer — there's something deeper going on than simply shedding a few pounds. To truly connect with your ideal client, it's good to be very clear on the very deepest WHY they want the transformation.

Okay so once you have your features and benefits, it's time to turn those benefits into bullets.

*What you want to do is take each benefit and make it a bullet —
but just the benefit part, not the feature.*

So using the above example, here's how I would turn it into a
bullet:

> 💜 Learn the top 10 foods to avoid (as well as
> 7 foods you MUST eat) to not only lose the
> weight, but to keep it off for good.

Now, I don't have the deepest benefit here (you don't need that
in every bullet) but I do have the losing weight and keeping it off
part. I also added numbers to make it more specific. I took the
benefit (losing weight and keeping it off) and turned it into a
stand-alone statement.

The third step is to polish it. I always go through my bullets again
and make sure they're really as strong as possible. So in this case I
may polish this bullet like so:

> 💜 Learn the top 10 so-called "healthy" foods
> to avoid (as well as 7 surprising foods you
> MUST eat) to not only lose the weight, but
> to keep it off for good.

See how I amped up not only the curiously factor but also the
word choices that imply you may be eating the foods you aren't

supposed to, as well as not eating the foods you should be — and that might be what's causing you to not lose the weight?

Here are a few more questions to ask yourself when you're polishing your bullets:

- Is it tangible enough? Would it help to add any specific numbers?

- Could I make it more of a mystery or amp up the curiosity factor?

- Is there a way to amp up the emotion?

- Is there a way to resolve the emotion?

- Are the words as strong and descriptive as they can be?

You may want to take a few days and run through that checklist a couple of times. What I've found is every time I've asked myself these questions, I can generally find some tweak to make the bullets even more powerful.

Wondering what to do with the features you've now removed from your benefit-driven bullets? Keep reading - we cover that next.

LOVE-BASED TIP: AMPLIFY EMOTIONS, NOT PAIN

Amplifying the emotion in your bullet can be extremely powerful. But amplifying the pain can push your copy into fear-based marketing if you're not careful.

So does this mean, as someone embracing love-based copy, you can't ever amplify the pain in the bullets?

Not necessarily. There are 2 ways you can do so, without being fear-based.

1. Don't go overboard. There are degrees of amplification, and a gentle amplification that is intended to remind your ideal prospects of their pain (rather trying to dive headfirst in the blame/shame/guilt game) is still love-based.

2. Use both techniques - amplify and resolve - in the same bullet. In other words — gently amplify the pain, and then immediately resolve it, so the overall feeling you leave your ideal prospects with is that of moving toward pleasure.

Here's how it would work:

> ❤ The number 1 mistake dieters make that will actually cause you to gain MORE weight (not to mention making you feel even more sluggish and sick)…and how one easy tweak can put your weight (and your health) right back on track.

So you amplify it first by adding the sluggish and sick part, and then you resolve it with the easy tweak part.

Chapter 8

PACKAGING YOUR GENIUS (I.E. YOUR LOVE-BASED OFFER)

So far we've covered:

- Preheads

- Headlines

- Subheads

- Beginnings

- Your Million-Dollar Story

- Your Big Picture Solution

- Drilling Down to the Details via Benefit-Driven Bullets

What's left?

You have to present your offer – which I call "Packaging Your Genius." This is a nice, tidy summary of what your ideal prospect will receive from you when she buys.

Once people have emotionally connected to you and your biz, they want to understand EXACTLY what you're selling, so they can see if it's a good fit (or not) for them. *So making a clear offer is crucial.*

Here's how the offer typically is laid out (and remember, all of this happens AFTER explaining the *value* of your offer via those benefit-driven bullets, so at this point, they should have a pretty good idea of what your product or service is all about and how it's going to tie into the transformation they want):

- The overview of the transformation

- What it includes (services delivery/features)

- Bonuses

- Cost/Justify Cost

- Guarantee

- Call to Action

Now, let's dig into each of these sections deeper.

OVERVIEW OF TRANSFORMATION
(covered in detail in Chapter 6):

Here, we're looking for just a paragraph or 2 - the big picture overview of the transformation/solution your ideal clients will experience.

Note: All of the following examples are from my "Why Isn't My Website Making Me Any Money?" sales letter (which you can check out in full right here: www.MichelePW.com/10easysteps)

Example:

> It's About Practical, No-Nonsense, Down-to-Earth, Tried-and-Tested Marketing Principals. It's About FINALLY Having a Solid Plan with Specific Action Steps Designed to Help You Transform Your Website into an Asset That Expands Your Reach, and Builds Your Biz.

SERVICE DELIVERY:

Specifically what they're going to get, i.e. 5 live calls, transcripts, worksheets, Q&A, coaching, etc. (Here's where you can talk about the features of your products or programs, what we covered in detail in Chapter 7).

Example:

- "Why Isn't My Website Making Me Any Money? diagnostic manual (40 pages jam-packed with ONLY the information you need) and training kit

BONUSES:

I'm not a big believer in a million bonuses — 3 bonuses (give or take) is plenty. And I also like the bonuses to directly tie into the offer itself. So, for instance, let's say you're a healer and you have a program teaching people how to heal themselves. Offering a bonus on how to use social media to promote your business isn't going to make any sense – but offering a bonus on using meditation as a healing method would.

You can also use bonuses to highlight parts of the offer that might otherwise get lost. For instance, you can pull out an open Q&A call as a bonus, a one-on-one laser-coaching call, a quickstart guide, or some sort of pre-work to highlight in the bonus section. (Quick tip: including the value of your bonus is a good idea, too.)

Example:

→ Bonus #1 – **A Complimentary Website Assessment with one of my trained website strategists.** Sometimes the absolute best thing you can do to achieve your website goal is get a pair of objective, trained eyes on it. That's why I'm including a thorough website assessment with one of my website strategists … to give you an opportunity to get professional feedback on what's working well AND what isn't, so you can finally start expanding your reach in a big way! ($197 value)

→ Bonus #2 – **2 Income Streams You Can Add to Your Business (And Increase Your Bottom Line) special report.** You could be leaving thousands of dollars on the table and not even know it! This special report walks you through hidden profit opportunities … and opportunities to reach more people … in your business. ($19.99 value)

→ Bonus #3 – **54 Low or No–Cost Ways to Get Traffic to Your Site (and 1 thing you should absolutely NOT do) special report.** Get a flood of new customers to your site (the ones who can't wait to do business with you!), without using pay-per-click or other methods that cost you a small fortune. ($47 value)

COST/ JUSTIFY COST:

First, clearly state the investment amount, and then justify the cost of the investment (yes, this IS necessary - people want to know they're getting a good deal). In a simple paragraph or so, cover things like how and/or why your offer will save your ideal prospect money and time, and make him more money, and then address the cost of NOT investing ... or all of the above. I go through this in more detail in the next chapter, which is all about objections (because money IS definitely an objection). But for this section, it's okay to gently remind your ideal prospect of his pain, while driving home the transformation he can expect. (Note: More on how to justify the cost in Chapter 9.)

Example:

Wondering now how much this is going to cost you?

First, I'd love for you to consider Why Isn't My Website Making Me Any Money? an investment rather than a cost. A cost is money you pay out without getting anything in return, whereas an investment earns your money back, many times over.

There is no question you could easily make thousands of dollars with the strategies and systems I've included in Why Isn't My Website Making Me Any Money? My personal clients pay me thousands to walk them through this EXACT system!

But I'm not going to charge you anywhere near that much. I've been there, remember? I know how stressful it is to have a gift to share, and to put up a website to share it … and then not convert any clients and not make any sales, and not understand why. And it's difficult to keep throwing money at something when you don't see the return on your investment — in terms of expanding your reach and growing your business (and your bank account!).

That's why I'm asking you to invest just $97.

For the price of a pair of new shoes or a business suit, or a dozen trips to Starbucks, you get access to thousands of dollars' worth of website marketing strategies you can implement NOW.

Imagine – learning EXACTLY why your website isn't converting your ideal prospects into ideal clients, AND having an action plan in place to transform it into a machine that expands your reach 24/7!

And as if this wasn't a good enough deal on its own (which I assure you, it is!), you're also getting a complimentary website assessment from a trained professional as part of your purchase. That alone is worth more than I'm asking you to invest in this product.

GUARANTEE:

If you are selling a product or a program, you definitely need some sort of guarantee. Keep in mind the point of a guarantee isn't to give people a way to take advantage of you. Instead, it's a way to take the risk off of the buyer and put it on the seller (which is you, the business person). Without a guarantee, your ideal clients are taking all the risk (they're the ones handing over a credit card without actually having the product in hand), so you want to try and mitigate that as much as possible.

Don't be afraid to make a strong guarantee either — studies have shown fewer people take advantage of longer guarantees than shorter guarantees. The thinking behind that is when the guarantee is short, people have a ticking clock in their heads and may even return something they haven't actually looked at very closely just to be on the safe side. When the guarantee is longer, people may just forget about it. Regardless, even if that sounds cynical, having a longer guarantee does feel more love-based, because you're giving them more opportunity to try your product or program out, before making a decision.

For services, offering a guarantee isn't so clear-cut, since your time is involved. Most people don't expect a guarantee with services, and my suggestion is to play it by ear and do what you feel most comfortable with.

Example:

> **Plus, you're covered by my full 1–year iron–clad 100% Money Back Guarantee:**
>
> I believe in over–delivering, so you are completely protected with my full 1–year iron–clad money-back guarantee. If you don't feel like you've made back 10 times your investment, I want you to return it for a full refund. (But please keep the bonus gifts as my "thank you" for giving it a try.)

> Basically, I'm taking all the risk here. You can try out all of my road–tested, proven strategies, action steps, everything, and see if they work for you. If they don't, just let me know and I'll refund your money. It's that simple.

CALL TO ACTION:

Ask people for their business with a specific call to action. Don't forget to clearly spell out what their next step should be — if you want them to buy something, then ask them to buy. If you want them to sign up for a free consultation, ask them to do that. What's important is you give clear and specific direction as to what you want them to do next.

Remember how, in Chapter 1, I talked about starting with the "end in mind" – and how the entire piece of copy should be written to support people in taking this next step? This is the place where you actually spell out what that next step is.

Example:

> Bottom line: Why Isn't My Website Making Me Any Money is for you if you're ready to expand your reach and deliver your message to a greater number of clients while growing your business and making more money.

So **NOW** are you ready?

(Followed by the "restate the offer box" — more on that in chapter 11.)

EXERCISE

Probably the easiest way to write the Packaging Your Genius section is to figure out what you want to say in each section and then flesh out copy.

So, to remind you, here are the sections again:

- The overview of the transformation (which you should already have from Chapter 6)

- What it includes (services delivery/features)

- Bonuses

- Cost/Justify Cost (note — you'll find more on this section in the next chapter)

- Guarantee

- Call to Action

First, jot down notes about what you want to cover for each of these sections. Then come back and flesh it out. (Use the examples and explanations provided to help you do this.)

LOVE-BASED TIP:
MAKE PEACE WITH MONEY

Money is one of the biggest issues I see conscious entrepreneurs grappling with.

It can take many forms — from undercharging and/or overdelivering, discounting, allowing clients to walk all over you, not owning your value, etc.

There are a lot of reasons behind why this happens, and this isn't the space to really sort it all out (I would probably need to write another book just on this topic to cover it adequately). But, I DO want to encourage you to make sure you're good with whatever price you're charging for the product/service you're selling.

If you're uncomfortable with the price you're asking — your ideal prospects will sense it. And they won't buy.

Now, that doesn't mean I want you to undercharge for whatever you're selling — that doesn't work either. If something looks like too good of a deal, people will be skeptical and won't buy. So, your price needs to reflect the value.

Once you know that value, then you just need to make sure YOU'RE good with it.

If you're not, if you feel uncomfortable or resistance when you think about the price, definitely do some work around it. There are a lot of great programs and books out there that can help you get comfortable around owning your value and stopping all of that undercharging or discounting or overdelivering, etc. and it may be the right move to look into that before you do a lot of promoting around your product. (Besides, getting through those money

blocks is a great way to significantly grow your business.)

Chapter 9
OBJECTIONS

So far we've covered:

- Preheads

- Headlines

- Subheads

- Beginnings

- Your Million-Dollar Story

- Your Big Picture Solution

- Drilling Down to the Details via Benefit-Driven Bullets

- Presenting Your Offer by Packaging Your Genius

Next up: objections.

No matter what you ask people to do — click on a link, give them your name and email address, request a consultation, buy something — they will have objections to doing it (even if it's something they really want to do!).

Typically when this happens, it means the mind has begun to take over. Before, you were tapping into emotions, which is what you need to do to inspire action. But, eventually, the minute you're actually getting ready to TAKE action, the mind decides to butt in and start protesting:

"Wait a minute — are you SURE you want to do this?" Then, it proceeds to give you a whole bunch of reasons why this isn't such a hot idea.

The bigger the action you want to take, the more pushback your mind is going to give you — which is typically why you end up with a longer online sales letter when you're going to charge more for a product.

So, how do you deal with objections? Meet them head first.

Look, the objections are there regardless, whether you talk about them or not. So if you don't talk about them, your ideal prospects won't have an answer to what their mind is telling them, and they'll just go away.

Now, if they don't have the objection, they'll still actually appreciate you bringing it up, and you'll come across as more credible and trustworthy.

There are 3 different types of objections — universal objections, specific objections and secret objections. Universal objections are objections everyone has anytime they are going to buy something

— which is money and time (unless you're buying shoes, then you won't have the time objection). Specific objections are those that relate to your specific industry and/or product. Secret objections are the objections your ideal clients are feeling but not talking about…and in many cases, not even admitting to themselves.

Let's start with the two universal objections.

Money — handle the objection about how much something costs by first telling people what the price is, and then justifying the price. (And this usually happens in the Packaging Your Genius section, which we talked about briefly in the last chapter, but here are a few more ways you can justify the price):

💜 Explain how this investment will help your ideal prospect make more money than what she pays you for your product or service. For instance: You're going to learn marketing strategy that will help you make thousands of dollars - and you're only going to pay a few hundred.

💜 Explain how this investment will help your ideal prospect stop losing money. This can work a couple different ways — you can talk about how he is losing opportunities or money because he doesn't have X. Or, you can talk about how he's wasting money because he doesn't have X — for instance, if you're a nutritionist you could cover the cost objection by talking about how, because your ideal prospect doesn't know the right foods to eat, he's spending a ton of money on over-the-counter drugs. But once he begins eating better, he'll likely be able to throw out all those pain medications and antacids.

💜 Ask your ideal prospect directly to think about what it's worth to have her pain solved: What would it be worth to you to have X taken care of? Now, you need to be careful you don't fall into shaming; you want to make it a legitimate question. What IS it worth to them to finally have the transformation? Maybe it's not worth the price of what you're selling to them — and if that's the case, then bless them and let them move on.

💜 Compare the price to something else your ideal clients are buying — for instance the whole "a cup of coffee a day" technique. "For the price of a cup of coffee for a month, you can have X."

What I like to do is use at least a couple of these techniques and weave them together in a couple of paragraphs. The idea here isn't so much to twist people's arms who aren't your ideal clients, but rather to tell the people who are that you really are giving them a good deal. (I'm assuming your product or service IS a good deal. People want to know they aren't being taken advantage of, and here, you're just letting them know they're not.)

Now, if you DO find you're in a situation where you feel like you need to twist someone's arm (like they say to you "I don't have the money" or "that's so expensive"), chances are it's because you haven't done your job.

Either you haven't priced your product or program correctly, or you haven't built enough value into your bullets.

The vast majority of time, when people say they don't have the money or they don't have the time, it's NOT because they don't have the money or time, it's because they're choosing not to spend it on your product or program. And if that's their choice, chances are it's because you didn't communicate the transformation and the "what's in it for them" clearly and compellingly enough. So, reviewing the lessons in Chapter 6 and 7 would be the best place to start.

Okay, so let's look at the time objection. (And just a quick note here: the time objection, along with the specific and secret objections, are often covered best in a Frequently Asked Questions section of your copy. Please see below for example.)

For some, time is considered more valuable than money because you can always make more money, but you can't make more time. So if you're selling something where people need to invest their time, it's typically a good idea to also justify that investment of time.

How do you do that? A couple of ways:

- Break the time commitment down for people. So, for instance, maybe it's an hour a week for the next 8 weeks, or 15 minutes a day for the next month, or some combination (an hour training per week plus 30 minutes for homework). If you can break it down like that, it won't feel so overwhelming.

💜 Explain how you can take the time now to learn how to XXX, which will save time later.

💜 Ask them if the result they want is worth the time commitment. Again, don't fall into shaming — make it a legitimate question and don't be attached to their answer.

Those are the two universal objections. Next, you want to move to specific objections — those that are specific to your product, service or industry.

In many cases, you'll already know what those objections are — for instance, you work with high-end corporate executives and you already know they highly value confidentiality and privacy, so you know you need to make it clear in your marketing materials that they will be completely protected when working with you.

But, what if you don't know them? Never fear — your ideal clients will tell you.

Typically, they'll tell you through the questions they ask. I'm not talking about questions like "Will the calls be recorded?" and "How long are the coaching sessions?" Those are feature-based. I'm talking about questions such as "Will your program cover this?" or "I have this problem, will your program help with that?"

I suggest keeping a record of all the questions you get, and then look for themes. The questions you hear over and over are actually objections — they want your program but they're on the fence and looking for something from you that will tip them one way or another.

I also suggest you handle the time objection, as well as all specific and secret objections, in a Frequently Asked Questions section in either emails or your actual marketing copy.

Finally, let's talk about secret objections.

Part of the reason these objections are secret is because they're embarrassing to your ideal client. Your ideal client is questioning herself — maybe she's bought other types of programs or products and failed (and the reason she failed is because she know in her heart that she didn't do the work for whatever reason) or she's worried she won't do the necessary work this time to succeed.

In other words, she's doubting herself.

In the traditional fear-based direct response copywriting approach, this was the most difficult objection to overcome because, at the end of the day, it's really about your ideal client's personal commitment to solving her own problem. It has absolutely nothing to do with you or your product/program. She can 100% believe in YOU — believe you're the real deal, your product or program works and others are getting great results from it. She may believe that she too would get great results IF she does the work.

But she doesn't know if she's up to doing the work.

So, in the fear-based approach, the only way to really "convince" someone to do the work is to steamroll over her objection and basically shame her or blame her or guilt her into doing it. Which, alas, could work. At least in the short-term, which means you get the initial sale.

But chances are very good these are also the people who will fail with your program too. They only bought because you made them feel bad about not buying, which means their head is full of "shoulds" around solving this problem. In other words, you didn't convince them to buy for all the "right" reasons, in a love-based way.

So, quite honestly, a better way to handle this objection IS the love-based way, which is by holding the space to challenge their belief that they won't do the work this time, but NOT twisting their arm. This way, if they realize they really aren't ready to do the work, you let them walk away, knowing they are not your ideal clients.

This is one of the trickiest areas to remain love-based, because it is a razor-thin line between challenging and shaming. But if you're truly coming from a place of abundance and love, you should be able to walk that line safely and comfortably.

EXAMPLE OF FREQUENTLY ASKED QUESTION SECTION:

Q: I don't have time for your program.

If you're answering in the typical fear-based way, the answer probably sounds something like this:

> A: Successful people make time for programs like this because they know it's going to change their life. If you don't feel like you can make the time, you're probably not ready to be successful yet.

You can feel how shaming that sounds, right?

Now, let's answer that in a love-based way:

> A: We're all in different paths on our journey and you're right, you may not be ready for this. And that's okay! We ALL procrastinate on doing the things we need to do in order to make a change when it's not the right time yet.
>
> But before you decide you're really not ready, just do me a favor and check in with yourself. Are you absolutely sure you don't have the time? Could you actually BE ready to change … but your fear is standing in your way?

> The best gift you can give yourself is to make
> a decision one way or another right now —
> staying on the fence only sucks your energy.
> If the answer is no, that's fine. If the answer
> is yes (even if you're scared of saying yes and
> what that means) know I'm super happy to be
> working with you and supporting you on your
> journey.

See the difference?

EXERCISE

The easiest way to conquer handling objections is to focus on one objection at a time. First money in the price justification section, then time, specific and secret objections in the FAQ section.

When you write the money and time objections, I would make sure you include multiple explanations to soothe your ideal client's concerns.

If you're selling a new product or program, clearly you won't have any specific objections for it, but you can include questions and objections you hear about your industry in general. The important thing is to get something out now, because you can always tweak and add questions or objections as you go along. Let the marketplace help you with your marketing — in other words, get it out there, even if it's imperfect, so you can get feedback from your ideal prospects and then make the necessary tweaks so it's the most powerful and compelling copy possible.

One other note — while money should always be its own section (part of Packaging Your Genius), and specific and secret objections are natural fits for the FAQ section, the time objection can go either way. You could have a couple paragraphs dedicated to that specific objection, OR you can integrate it into the FAQ section, if it flows better.

LOVE-BASED TIP: GIVE YOUR IDEAL CLIENTS SPACE

I touched on this in the section about secret objections above, but one key to writing love-based copy around objections is to create a safe space for your ideal prospects to feel into their objections, and figure out if they are truly ready for change.

This is the decision place — where people are deciding yes or no.

And below is a good foundation to follow if you want it to sound love-based:

> Is living in the pain of your current situation
> greater than the pain of spending money and
> time to fix it now? Or are you not quite ready for
> the solution?

When your ideal prospects arrive at this place in your copy, YOU have your own choice to make. What's most important to you? Is it getting the sale above all costs? Does the end justify the means? Do you have the "It's okay, I know my program will help them so if I just push them here a bit, and twist their arm a bit, they'll be better off taking my program than not doing it" mentality?

Or, are you willing to give your ideal prospects the space to make up their own mind about what they truly want and what's best for them, even if it means less money in your pocket?

Remember, direct response copy is NOT about twisting people's arms — it's about creating a buying environment where people are able to figure out what they want and then take action (or not) to get it.

If you don't create a compelling buying environment, they'll never take a crucial pause at this place in your copy to go inside themselves to see if this is a true yes or no, for them. (And even though it may not feel like it in the moment, many times allowing those people who aren't ideal clients to walk away at this point in your copy actually works out better for you, too.)

And keep in mind that the "no" can be just as important as the "yes" — JUST as long as the no comes AFTER they really thought about it — not because your message was just so "meh" or weak that they forgot about it the moment they clicked away.

So, before you write the objections, take a moment to pause, breathe, and create that safe space in your mind, first, for your ideal prospects to make the right decision for them. And just know, when you handle the objections in a way that allows them to make the right decision for them, they're actually making the

right decision for everyone — including you.

Chapter 10

WHAT ELSE DO YOU NEED? OTHER ESSENTIAL ELEMENTS TO COMPLETE YOUR MARKETING PIECES

So far we've covered

- Preheads

- Headlines

- Subheads

- Beginnings

- Your Million-Dollar Story

- Your Big Picture Solution

- Drilling Down to the Details via Benefit-Driven Bullets

- Presenting Your Offer by Packaging Your Genius

- Addressing Objections

Now, it's time to talk about other essential elements you need for compelling love-based copy.

Social Proof/Testimonials — It's pretty difficult to sell much of anything without including testimonials of some sort, especially now, when marketing skepticism is at an all-time high (and probably isn't going to drop again any time soon).

Of course, people are ALSO skeptical of testimonials, so you'll need to keep that in mind as you collect them.

If done right, testimonials can help inspire your ideal prospects in a few ways. They:

- Show people you're credible — the online world can be a scary place. Just because someone has set up a website and a shopping cart doesn't mean they're an actual honest person with a reputable business who will deliver what they promised, and not steal your identity. If you include testimonials from people who have purchased products and services from you and are happy enough to publicly say it, that can help reassure people you are who you say you are.

- Prove the results of your product or service better than anything you could say yourself. It's one thing for you to tout how great your product or service is; it's quite another to have someone else describe the great results they got themselves, because of it. People are far more likely to believe what other people are saying about you than what you're saying about you.

- Help sooth specific objections. Everyone believes their problem is "unique" — yes they know other people struggle with the same problem, but other people don't have their specific life circumstances to contend with.

For instance, let's say you're in the weight loss business. Your ideal prospects may say things like "Well, I get that other people may be able to lose weight with you, but those people don't have kids and work a full-time job like I do." So, you include testimonials from your clients who have kids and work a full-time job.

That makes a more compelling case then if you simply told them "Yes it will still work for you."

Now, if you want your testimonials to actually do some heavy lifting for you, you need something more than "Jane Doe is awesome!"

In the Exercise section below, I share some of my tips for collecting and writing testimonials (I'm including an effective testimonial-writing formula, too!).

Multi-Media Elements — The more ways people can interact with you, the more "real" you'll become to them, which means they'll become more likely to "know, like and trust" you. (Which is important because remember, people prefer doing business with people they know, like and trust.)

That's why adding audio or video can increase conversions. (Conversions refers to the number of people out of 100 who take action. So, if 40 people out of 100 opt in for a free report, you have a 40% conversion.)

Now, for the most part, audio only isn't going to move the needle as much as a video — but that doesn't mean audio only can't be an important part of your marketing. Podcasts and online radio shows are still hot — and people like loading up a bunch of different podcasts and recordings to listen to while they're exercising, driving, or otherwise multi-tasking. But for the purposes of the content on your websites and sales pages, video is better than audio.

But, just because you're putting a video up does NOT mean it needs to be all that long. *Your video should be as long as you can hold your audience's attention — which means, if you're like most people, only a minute or two.*

BONUS: Here's a basic script for a sales video:

- Introduce yourself

- Talk about who your ideal client is, and what her pain is (but do it in a way so you're talking TO them not AT them).

- Explain how your solution can solve that pain

💗 Invite them to read more, get all the details, and join you

The key word to keep in mind when creating a video script is to make it BRIEF. Again, we're only talking about a minute or two, which is only a few hundred words (depending on how fast you talk). So you don't have a lot of time — which is fine because remember all you're trying to do is have them get a sense of who you are so they get a feel as to whether or not they are comfortable moving forward with you.

Graphics — Let's start with a few truths about graphics, so you can make educated decisions about what to spend your money on.

💗 A professional picture of you — this is a big YES. Not only should you hire a professional photographer, but for all you ladies, getting some help with your wardrobe choice, hair style and makeup is also a must.

This is part of helping your ideal prospects get to know who you are (yes – it's the "know, like, trust" thing again). Plus, with all the different places to post your picture online, having a few good ones is even more critical.

💗 An appealing, professional page – while it's not necessary to spend thousands of dollars on a beautiful, custom website or graphics, you also don't want it to look homemade. What you need is a nice, professional website, and with the templates out there (WordPress is one that comes to mind), it is possible for you to do it yourself. (Tip: The only aspect of design you may want to spend some money on is a custom banner and maybe some help with the color palette.)

- Logo — I'm not sold on the theory that you need an expensive logo. Sure, a logo is helpful, but if you're just starting out and on a tight budget, you can definitely skip the logo, or just go with a low-cost option.

And with the money you save on unnecessary graphics and logos, you can afford this much more important feature:

- Mobile friendly – this is a MUST. I've seen numbers as high as 70% of visitors using tablets and phones, so if your website or sales letters aren't mobile friendly (and mobile friendly means your online pages format themselves for whatever device your visitor is using), then your visitors are struggling to view your pages. Needless to say, they aren't going to spend a lot of time on them, when they can find a different mobile-friendly site to help them, instead. (Note: If you don't know how to set your site up so that it's mobile friendly, don't worry- hiring someone to do that for you is pretty affordable.)

So, to summarize, you definitely need great headshots and a nice, professional, attractive website and sales letters, but spending thousands on graphics or logos is something you can most definitely skip.

EXERCISE

I've designed this next exercise to help you write and collect powerful testimonials.

Let's start with how to write them.

First off, you want to go deeper than simply having people share how amazing you are, or how much they love you. People aren't investing in your products and services because you're amazing; they're investing because they want the transformation you promise, and they're convinced you'll deliver it.

Which means having your testimonials tell a story – having them show your ideal prospects HOW you provided a solution to their problem — can be so powerful.

(Hence, the "I think she's awesome" testimonials don't carry a lot of weight.)

Okay so how do you write testimonials that tell a story?

Here's a template you can follow:

- Introduction — who they are and what their circumstances are (BRIEFLY — just a sentence or two)

- Problem/Pain — what their life was like before they worked with you

💜 Why they decided to invest

💜 What results they got from working with you

Now, most testimonials are pretty short — a paragraph or two — so each one of those sections should be concise.

Ok, so how do you actually get testimonials?

Well, probably the easiest way is to write a testimonial for them and send it to them for editing. You can ask them specific questions beforehand (either verbally or an email) to draw out the information you need. For instance, you can ask:

What was your life like before you invested in my program/product/service?

Why did you decide to invest with me?

What results did you get?

How is your life different now than it was then?

Once you get the information, it's just a matter of cleaning up what they say to make it flow better (and maybe shorten it), and you're ready to go.

As much as possible, you want the testimonials to be "real" and believable — so make sure you ask permission to use the person's name, city/town, and picture (if possible). Video testimonials are better yet, if you can get them.

Lastly, you don't just need to ask people who have actually hired you — you can also ask people who you've helped for free. Maybe it's your hair dresser or one of your friends you coached, and they got fabulous results. Just as long as your offering helped them and they're willing to tell people about, feel free to ask them for a testimonial, as well.

LOVE-BASED TIP: WATCH THE HYPE

So you already know, since you're at this point in the book, to stay away from exaggeration and hype. Now, while this is pretty good advice to follow throughout all your marketing copy, testimonials are one of those places where it can be really easy to slip into exaggeration, even if you don't mean to.

Remember, if you slip into too much hype, folks may end up having trouble either believing the testimonial at all, or believing they can get the same results. If they start saying things like "Well, sure that person could get those results because they probably don't have kids like I do," then you've probably lost them.

If your client is on video just singing your praises without talking about the transformation she experienced, you can probably still use it because their passion and sincerity will come through, but if you put it in written form, it probably won't translate as well (in other words, people will think it's just a bunch of hype).

Part 3

PUTTING IT ALL TOGETHER

Chapter 11

APPLYING THE SYSTEM TO EMAILS, SALES LETTERS, OPT-IN PAGES, WEBSITES AND DIRECT MAIL

Now that we've gone through all the basic elements of writing love-based sales copy, the next step is to show you how to plug those elements into the different promotional pieces you'll likely need for your business.

I've organized this chapter in a way that outlines the various sections to include in your copy, in the typical order you would find them, for each marketing piece. (In essence, I've created a template for you for each marketing piece that corresponds to what you learned in the previous chapters.) And if you've been working on the exercises as you've moved through the book (hint hint) you'll now be able to simply "plug" your copy in to the different marketing pieces. Once you've done that, all you'll need to do is smooth out the writing, add transitions and voila! Your copy is done!

Sales letters (also known as long copy sales letters) – Again, these are those long pages you scroll down forever looking for the price and likely think to yourself "Does anyone actually read these?" (Answer: Yes.)

If you want to sell a product or program less than $2,000 online, this is the marketing piece you use. Along with incorporating all the different elements we covered in this book, in the order in which we covered them, you'll also want to intersperse testimonials throughout, and add a video to the top of the page.

Here are the elements to be sure to include:

- Prehead

- Headline

- Subhead

- Beginning

- Your Million-Dollar Story

- Your Big Picture Solution

- Drilling Down to the Details via Benefit-Driven Bullets

- Presenting Your Offer by Packaging Your Genius

- Addressing Objections (Reminder: you may want to do this in the Frequently Asked Questions section)

Now, there's an additional section you'll want to include on a sales letter after the objections, where you Restate the Offer.

Restating the Offer is usually its own box, written in first person from the ideal prospects' viewpoint. ("YES! I can't wait to start losing weight with Jane's weight loss program.")

Here, you briefly restate everything included in your offer, as presented in your Packaging Your Genius section. The idea is to have them reiterate what they're getting, to ensure they are completely clear in their expectations. Using mostly bullet points, you want to include:

- Price and payment options (if you're offering payment plans)

- Features/Service delivery

- Bonuses

- Guarantee

- Clear Call to Action

Example:

> Yes, Michele! I'm ready to transform my website into a marketing machine that works to turn ideal prospects into ideal clients 24/7, leveraging my time, energy, and resources — while getting my message out in the world! I understand that for my investment of $97, I receive:

→ **Why Isn't My Website Making Me Any Money? manual / diagnostic tool**

→ **Bonus #1 – A Complimentary Website Assessment with a trained website strategist** to give me a fresh, objective look at what's working and what isn't. ($197 value)

→ **Bonus #2 – 2 Income Streams You Can Add to Your Business (And Increase Your Bottom Line) special report,** so I can stop leaving thousands of dollars on the table. ($19.99 value)

→ **Bonus #3 – 54 Low or No–Cost Ways to Get Traffic to Your Site (and 1 thing you should absolutely NOT do) special report.** ($47 value)

And I understand I'm protected by your full 1-year, 100% Iron Clad, Money-Back Guarantee:

> If I don't feel like I've made back 10 times my investment, I can return it for a full refund. (But I'll get to keep the bonus gifts as your "thank you" for giving it a try.)
>
> **Add To Cart**
>
> VISA MasterCard DISCOVER AMERICAN EXPRESS PayPal

You'll also likely want to end your sales letter with a P.S. (or even up to 3 P.S.') As the second most frequently read portion of a sales letter (after the headline), this is an excellent place to mention the biggest objections again, touch upon the pain again (don't agitate - just gently remind them if they choose not to take action, which is perfectly valid, the pain will still be there), or reiterate a desirable bonus.

In order to really drive each of these main points home, it's important to only cover one idea per P.S. (So, for example, one P.S. could cover the time objection, one could touch on a specific pain point, and the third could restate a valuable and desirable bonus).

Example:

P.S. If you're thinking you don't have time to implement what you learn in **Why Isn't My Website Making Me Any Money?** then you might need it more than you realize! When you discover the truth behind why your website isn't working for you, and follow my easy, step-by-step guidance for implementing powerful marketing strategies, your website works for you 24/7, which frees up tons of time and supercharges your productivity. Why wait any longer to maximize your efficiency? **Order your copy of Why Isn't My Website Making Me Any Money?** today.

P.P.S. You know there are people out there whose lives you can transform … and when you use the foundational marketing principles in **Why Isn't My Website Making Me Any Money?** you can FINALLY reach *more* of them. Stop wishing you could find more of your ideal clients, and let your website do it for you. Expand your reach and share your brilliant message, starting today. Order your copy now.

P.P.P.S. Remember, along with your copy of **Why Isn't My Website Making Me Any Money?** you receive a bonus website assessment from one of my trained coaches (value $250). This means you get a second set of eyes – expert, objective, highly trained eyes – on your website, and a dose of personalized advice about how you can improve it. Order today.

Websites — a collection of pages that cover multiple areas of your business. I like to think of a website as an online showroom — if you had a brick and mortar store, you would likely have a showroom where your ideal prospects could come in, sit down, and chat with you about whether your products or services are a good fit for them, right?

Well, your website is a virtual version of your showroom, where your ideal prospects and clients can come in, look around, and even sit down and have a conversation with you. (And, yes, your copy on your promotional materials IS a two-way conversation; I'll get into that more in the next chapter.)

Now, there's typically a lot less copy on a website page than a sales letter, so while you will cover many of the same elements, you'll spend far less time on each of them than you would on a sales letter. So, for instance, on your home page, your million-dollar story may end up only being a sentence or two. (Note: You also don't need to include every single section.)

One thing to keep in mind is there are MANY website templates out there, so it's difficult to give you a specific template for each page, but here are some ideas for the content each page might include (hopefully, you can fit these sections into the template of your choice):

Home page — (Remember to keep all of these sections pretty short – your home page copy should be around 300-500 words, total, generally speaking. You may want to include a Welcome video at the top of the page, and definitely intersperse testimonials throughout not only your home page copy, but also throughout the entire site.)

- Headline (optional prehead and subhead)

- Beginning (touch on pain points)

- Your Million-Dollar Story (only a sentence or two. You can share it more fully on an "About" page, if you'd like.)

- Your Big Picture Solution

- Call to Action. Keep in mind the main Call to Action for your website should be to inspire your ideal prospects to opt in/give you their name and email address for a free gift. This is especially true for your home page — which is why many home pages have multiple opt-in opportunities for your gift. Minimally, you'll probably want to include an opt-in form directly on the banner of your page, in the upper left hand corner (as that's the first place people will naturally look) and then repeat the CTA again at the end of the home page copy. I like to have a transition sentence, like — "Ready to get started? Download my FREE gift, "TITLE," right now, and begin (fill in benefit) today.

Products pages – For each of your products, programs and/or events, you'll need a Products page – also known as a sales letter. (See above.)

Services pages – Generally speaking, because services are higher-priced than products, you don't use a sales letter to make the sale. Services are more effectively sold via phone call — either a complimentary strategy session or a regular sales call — which is why you typically don't list any pricing on these pages. Your Services pages, then, might look like this:

- Headline (optional prehead and subhead)

- Beginning (touch on pain points)

- Your Big Picture Solution

- Drilling Down to the Details via Benefit-Driven Bullets

- Call to Action — Call or email to set up a complimentary strategy session, to see if the particular service offered is a good fit for them.

About page —

💗 Your Million-Dollar Story – This is where you get to share the "long" version of your personal story. Or, you may want to have the shorter, more professional bio first and then the longer, more personal story after that. If you don't include your professional bio, you may want to include experiences, trainings, etc. that exemplify how you can relate to your ideal prospect, and how/why you're best-qualified to help them at the end of your million-dollar story.

Opt-in pages – When you land on a page that asks you to enter your name and email address in return for something FREE, you're likely looking at an opt-in page. Often, opt-in pages are used to offer free access to a training call, webinar or video training, a free report, book or audio, or to something delivered via email, like a 5-part e-course.

Like many online tools, opt-in pages have evolved over the years. Right now, it appears less is more — so a typical opt-in page looks like this:

💗 Headline — While headlines are always important on any piece of copy, they take on an extreme importance for opt-in pages, due to the limited amount of copy on the page. If you're using a template (like Lead Pages, for example), you may only have space for a headline, graphic, a couple sentences about what the freebie is, and the call to action (which is entering your name and email). Note: In some cases, the headline ends up being the title of the freebie — so it may be the title of the eBook or training call, in which case (and if template space allows), you can add a prehead or subhead to help round out the details.

- Beginning — IF you have this, it's pretty short and mostly focuses on identifying your ideal client, often through a few short pain points.

- Drilling Down to the Details via Benefit-Driven Bullets — Again, IF you have this, keep it short - no more than 3 or 4 bullets, total.

- If you're asking someone to give you their name and email, you probably instinctually want to tell them a little about yourself, to further instill the value of your offer, right? While this makes perfect sense, including your Million Dollar Story on this page will make it too long. Instead, consider including your bio and maybe a couple of testimonials AFTER the opt-in copy itself, at the bottom of the page.

(Side note — while I'm a big believer in testing, I'm an especially big believer in testing opt-in pages. A simple tweak can make a huge difference in your opt-in conversions. I'll cover testing more in the next chapter.)

Emails — Emails are an essential part of selling your products and services online. They're the only marketing piece that reaches out and touches your ideal prospects directly where they are right in that moment. The other promo pieces we've touched on (sales letters, websites, opt in pages) require your ideal prospects to take action in order to find and read them.

There are lots of ways to use emails in your marketing campaigns, such as:

* When you're launching a product or program (or anytime you want to let your community know you're selling something).

* As an auto-responder series (this is a series of emails written in advance and then loaded into an email program that will then automatically send them out for you (ie. 1Shopping Cart, Constant Contact, Mail Chimp, etc.). AR series are great for things such as list-warming and encouraging an initial purchase when someone first joins your list. You can provide them with immediate content, and make them an initial offer, all with a completely automated AR series.

* Regular email correspondence to your community to continue to nurture your relationship with them.

- A post-purchase email sequence (usually an AR series) to help deliver the purchased content and for continued customer service.

Since there are so many different ways to use emails in your marketing efforts, it's difficult to give you a specific template, but here are some tips to get you started:

An email is an electronic letter, so it's more personal than other mediums. That's why a "warm" message can work really well here. Keep in mind you are NOT trying to make the sale in an email — for the most part, your goal is just to get people to click on a link (whether it's to an opt in page, a download page, a sales letter, etc.). In other words, all you really have to do in an email is get the click.

Typical email structure:

- Subject line – Think of this as your "headline." Remember how a headline is the most read portion of a sales letter? Combined with the identification of the sender, the subject line is what will either encourage your recipients to actually read your email … or to click away.

- Beginning — Keep this fairly short. Opening with something vulnerable and/or personal can work well here. You can also lead with urgency (like if you're having a sale, you can include the date/time the sale ends).

💜 Call to Action/Link — You'll want to make sure your first CTA and link appears fairly high up on the page. I like to have it above the fold (imagine holding the document in your hands, folded in thirds. The first link should be above the first fold to encourage those who prefer not to read – because they're already ready to click – to do so).

💜 Your Big Picture Solution/Drilling Down to the Details via Benefit-Driven Bullets — depending on what you're looking to do with your email, you may want to include either the Big Picture Solution, or the benefit-driven bullets, or both. But remember, keep it pretty short.

💜 Final Call to Action/Link

💜 Your Signature

💜 P.S. — This is a great place to overcome an objection, offer a bonus tip, restate the urgency, or include a testimonial. Be sure to include a link in these, as well, to make it easy for people to click.

Direct Mail — This includes anything mailed, such as a postcard, letter, or brochure. These pieces can vary greatly in terms of length — I've seen everything from a couple of paragraphs on a postcard to a 20 page sales letter mailed through the postal system.

A few tips:

Postcard:

- Headline (optional prehead and subhead)

- Beginning — Keep this fairly short. Opening with something vulnerable and/or personal can work well here. You can also lead with urgency (like if you're having a sale, you can include the date/time the sale ends).

- Your Big Picture Solution/Drilling Down to the Details via Benefit-Driven Bullets — depending on what you're looking to do with your postcard, you may want to include either the Big Picture Solution, or the benefit-driven bullets, or both. But remember, keep it pretty short.

- Call to Action

Note: If you want to mail a sales letter, follow the sales letter template earlier in this chapter and just adjust the copy as needed to fit the desired length.

Chapter 12 — Advanced Tips

Once you've mastered the basics, you'll definitely want to begin looking at ways to polish your copy and take it to the next level. That's what this chapter is all about – extra tips and strategies for refining your Love-Based marketing materials.

Without further ado, below is a potpourri of advanced-level tips and strategies to help you get even better results with your copy.

Tip 1: Test, test and then test some more. Okay, so maybe you don't have to go THAT crazy. But the point here is the first piece of copy you put out there — whether it's an email or a sales page or website — is probably NOT going to be your absolute best. In fact, I can pretty much guarantee there's always room for improvement.

But you won't know that unless you actually put it out there and let the market give you feedback, right?

So there are 2 lessons here:

#1 – It does NOT have to be perfect. You just need a solid piece of copy (which will now be much easier for you to write, having gone through this book!). So, don't stress about your first draft and, whatever you do, DON'T feel bad if it turns out to be a flop. (That's the beauty of testing and tweaking.) It's nothing personal if people don't take your desired action, and it doesn't mean the Universe is trying to send you some sort of message that you're not on the right track with whatever you're selling. It's simply an opportunity to improve your copy, and your marketing.

#2 – Evaluate the stats. Once your copy is published online and you begin driving traffic to it (or you start sending emails), watch the stats. You should track:

💜 How many people actually saw your copy

💜 How many actually took the action you were inviting them to take

Once you've done that, you have a baseline, and can then go back and test different versions of the copy, to see if you can improve on those initial stats.

Wondering what to test?

💜 Headlines – Try a completely new headline, tweak the wording of the existing headline, add urgency, etc.

💜 Subject lines – Vary the length, ask a question, touch on a pain point … try something new.

💜 Your Big Picture Solution — Make sure your solution actually solves your ideal clients' specific problem. (Remember how I talked about being too "mushy" in your offer in Chapter 6. You may want to double-check to ensure you're using benefit-driven bullet points, Also, be sure you've identified your ideal prospects' pain/ biggest problem correctly.)

- **Don't ask a piece of copy to do more than its job.**
  Remember how I talked about "starting with the end in mind?" back in Chapter 1? This is a continuation of that — along with getting really clear about the ONE action you want your ideal clients to take, you also cannot ask (or expect) a piece of copy to do more than its job.

So, for instance, an email's job is to get the click. If you're selling a product, you send out an email with the sole purpose to entice your reader to click on the link, so the sales page can do the heavy lifting. It's the sales page's job to get them to buy.

An opt-in page's job is to convince people to give you their name and email address, in exchange for your free gift.

Facebook posts, Twitter tweets and other social networking copy should also be focused on getting the click, not the sale.

If you ask a single piece of copy to do too much, all you're likely to do is muddle your message, which will result in your ideal prospects not taking any action, besides going away.

- **Soft Approach to Selling** — Copywriting is often described as "salesmanship in print," so it makes sense that tactics that work well in face-to-face selling also work well in copy.

One such tactic is what I like to think of as a version of seeding.

Seeding is when you work the benefits of what you're selling into content. Or, you use the benefit to make a point, or answer a question, etc.

For example: You're hosting a content-based training, you say something like, "This is just one example of a "healthy" food that can actually make you fat! I cover 10 more in my 'TITLE' program."

Here's how seeding would look in copy, when you use benefits to strengthen the selling aspect, while keeping it "soft" so it doesn't sound fear-based (Note: The following paragraph can be used as a transition to encourage people to click on a link:)

> Here's where you can read real-life case studies from other entrepreneurs who have used my system to make big bucks, while making a big difference.

That's not a bad paragraph. But if you want to make it stronger, consider this:

> Here's where you can read real-life case studies from heart-centered entrepreneurs just like you who have used my proven system to make big bucks, while making a big difference.

So, as you can see, I added the following:

- "heart-centered" (which acts as a reminder of who this system is for)

- "just like you" (this is a great way to talk about a "secret" objection your ideal clients may have, which is that they won't succeed – "people just like you have gotten great results, so you can too" overcomes that objection)

- "proven" before system (again, as a gentle reminder that the system WORKS, since people tend to invest their time, money and energy in systems that WON'T waste their time/money/energy)

This is what I mean by seeding — slip in a few extra descriptive words into your copy to remind them who your offer is for, how it will help them (like it's helped likeminded entrepreneurs) and to soothe their concerns or overcome their objections.

Now, for those of us who aren't born sales people, this probably isn't a natural skill. So, what I would encourage you to do is after you write your copy, go through it again with a careful eye, paying specific attention to areas where you can strengthen the copy by adding those benefit-rich words and phrases.

- **Voice** – It's important that your copy "sound" like you, right? When it does, it increase the "know, like, trust" factor, and when your clients know, like, and trust you, they're more likely to buy.

So, there are two thing to consider when it comes to your "writing voice":

The second applies if you'd rather work with a copywriter, to help him/her effectively write in your voice.

Let's start with scenario one.

I have yet to see any decent tutorial or course focused on strengthening your writing voice (there is a book out there about adding your personality in your writing but I thought it was dreadful so I'm not going to recommend it) which makes me think:

> → A. It's not possible to teach it

> → B. No one has taken any time to figure it out

> → C. It's really an easy, obvious thing (Duh! Just write more!)

As much as I agree that, as a rule, people overcomplicate things, the fact that we have art school and music school and acting school and can somehow train people in other forms of art (but not writing) feels suspect to me. That said, I've cobbled together some tips I myself have used (influenced by the teachings of those other art/music/acting schools), and you can find those articles in the Appendix. I've included additional resources and exercises in the accompanying workbook, as well (which you can download at

LoveBasedCopywritingBook.com/workbook if you haven't already done so).

Scenario 2: I encourage you to work with a copywriter who has experience writing in her clients' voice. How will you know? Ask her. And ask her for samples of her work. You should be able to "hear" the different voices in the samples provided, if she is skilled.

Note: My own Love-Based Copywriting and Marketing Company has an entire process and system in place to better assist us in capturing our clients' voice. Interested? See the end of this book for more information about how we can write your copy for you.

- **2-Way Conversations** — Any piece of writing is actually a two-way conversation that occurs in the mind of the reader. As he reads, the reader responds to the copy in his mind – asking and answering questions as he goes.

So, if we were take this one step further, when you sit down to write copy, try and anticipate what questions your ideal prospects will form in their heads as they read, and be sure to provide the answers as you go.

Now, there is no question this is a more advanced copywriting technique, so don't beat yourself up if you struggle with it. But, it can be very effective when done correctly, so it's definitely worth the effort, if you're up to it.

- **Psychological Triggers and Emotions** — In my first Love-Based Copywriting book ("Love-Based Copywriting Method: The Philosophy Behind Writing Copy That Attracts, Inspires and Invites"), I focus quite a bit on psychological triggers, so I'll only give you the basics here.

In a nutshell, buying is an emotion-based experience (when you get right down to it, convincing people to do anything is an emotion-based experience). That means you need to tap into that emotion (pain, fear, anxiety, overwhelm, frustration, etc.), to get your desired result.

Psychological triggers are triggers that exist deep within us, and they relate to basic human needs for survival (food, water, shelter, belonging to a community, family preservation, etc.). They've been around, keeping us alive, since the days we lived in caves and ran from saber-toothed tigers. So, when you tap into those triggers, you're likely tapping into a deep psychological need we ALL have as humans. This works, because again, you're meeting your ideal prospect where she is right now, by acknowledging these triggers.

As you can probably tell, psychological triggers and emotions go hand-in-hand. So when you write sales copy, you definitely need to tap into both.

The question then becomes, will you do so in a fear or love-based way?

If you choose love-based, keep in mind people WANT those deep-rooted needs satisfied, so you're not doing anything wrong by giving them the option of letting you help them with those needs.

It becomes fear-based when you start trying to manipulate people into buying from you no matter the cost or regardless if it's the right move for them (I know you know the difference). If you want more on this topic, I would invite you to check out the first Love-Based Copy book.

Chapter 13 — What's Next?

Now that we've walked through the principle building blocks of the love-based copywriting system, the last step is to implement these principles into all of your marketing and copywriting.

Hopefully, when you started this book, you had a copywriting project in mind, and you focused on it as you completed the exercises in each chapter. If so, you're now ready to organize the exercises into the proper order, and use the templates in Chapter 11 to smooth and polish up the writing, add transitions and testimonials, and BOOM! You're good to go.

Then, every time you approach a new copywriting project — whether it's writing an email, a sales page for a new program or re-writing your website — circle back to this book and let the exercises help walk you through each piece.

Depending on where you are now and where you want to go, I've put together a collection of resources to help you further your love-based journey in the Resources section, so be sure to check that out, too.

Lastly, just remember you always have a choice. You can choose to market yourself with love or with fear.

And imagine how powerful it could be, if more of us choose love!

Not only could we transform the direct response copywriting industry, but we could also transform the way we conduct business - and even our entire world.

That's when we know we've truly made a difference.

Love and success,
Michele PW

Appendix —
Improve Your Writing Voice

5 WAYS TO ADD YOUR PERSONALITY TO YOUR WRITING

One of the fastest ways to transform your website and promotional materials into a client-attracting magnet is to add more of your personality into your writing.

(And yes, this still applies even if the vision you have for your business is bigger than yourself. You still want your personality to shine through the writing, because people want to do business with people they can relate to - not faceless, nameless corporations.)

Now, there are a few ways to successfully add more personality to your writing, including through things like branding and graphics. But what I want to focus on is how to do it through words.

Remember, the stronger your personality shows through your writing, the more loyal your customers and clients will be, and the more money you'll ultimately make.

So, here are 5 ways to add your personality to your writing:

1. **Read more.** The more you read, the more you'll learn how to express yourself in writing. Not only will you learn by example (especially if you read things by writers with very strong

personalities) but you'll start to absorb ways to express yourself using words that you'll be able to incorporate into your own writing.

2. **Write more.** Sorry, there's no getting around it! The more you do something, the better you'll get at it (and yes, that includes writing). Start a blog, write articles for your website, write letters to your friends ... it doesn't matter what you write - just start writing.

3. **Keep a journal.** I know - more writing? Yes, but this is a different kind of writing. It's more like exercising (okay, maybe that's not a great analogy either). Basically, journaling works because it gives your muse a way to "come out and play." And the more you can access your muse, the easier it will be to bring your personality out while you're writing.

Now, I used the word "journal" deliberately. That's because I want you to get out a pen and paper and start writing. Yes, I want you writing by hand. No computers. Something magical happens when you write by hand versus type. As for what to write, it truly doesn't matter – go with whatever comes up. (Staring at a blank page with zero ideas? Write "I have nothing to say" until you find you DO have something to say. Trust me – this works.) Do this regularly, and you'll be amazed at how much easier it gets to bring your personality into your writing.

4. **Read out loud.** This is a trick borrowed from actors. They read things out loud all the time, so they can hear their breathing,

phrasing, etc. This is a great way to find your actual "voice," which you then can transfer to writing.

And by the way, you don't have to read things *you've* written, for this to help. Read novels and nonfiction and articles and anything that strikes your fancy. And really listen to how you say the words. Everyone reads things differently, because you add your own personality into the reading, and that is what can translate into your writing.

5. **Write in other people's voice.** This is a trick borrowed from artists. When they learn to paint, they paint in the style of other great artists. By studying how other people paint, they pick up and practice other techniques. They incorporate what works with their style, and abandon what doesn't. An added bonus: By studying other people's styles, you'll start to be able to break down your own style, and thus you'll also better understand how to strengthen it.

Here's how to apply this technique to your writing: First, choose a writer whose style resonates with you. Next, copy a passage they wrote word-for-word. (You might want to do this a few times, actually.) Then write something original, but in their style. Keep practicing until writing in their style becomes second nature.

IMPORTANT: This is strictly a writing exercise. Don't try and copy other people's writing styles and pass them off as your own. Not only will it come across as inauthentic and likely turn off your target market, but depending on what you do, you could end up in legal trouble, too.

Even if you only incorporate a few of these tips, you should start to see a shift in your own writing. Before you know it, your personality will be shining through, and with it, you'll start to see more clients, more sales and more profits.

3 TIPS TO IMPROVE YOUR WRITING RHYTHM

As a professional copywriter, I do a lot of writing, sure. But I also look at a lot of writing, and one of the things I've noticed that sets the good/great writers apart from the "so-so" writers is the use of rhythm.

What I mean by rhythm is how the writing sounds. The rhythm of the words and sentences. It's a subtle aspect of writing, one not normally talked about, but that doesn't lessen its importance.

Unfortunately, rhythm is also tough to teach (which is probably why it isn't talked about very much). It's something felt deep inside, like it is with music. It isn't as straightforward as pointing out a grammatical error. What makes it tougher is that everyone has his/her own style and unique rhythm. However, the following three tips can help get you started thinking about your own writing rhythm, and how to improve it.

1. **Watch out for long sentences.** In fact, you might want to consider avoiding them altogether.

There's nothing inherently wrong with long sentences. And there are times where longer sentences are necessary (see next tip — but note I said longer and not long). The problem is that long sentences have a tendency to turn into flabby sentences.

Think of a sentence as an eel. The longer it gets, the more slippery and elusive it becomes. Long sentences are sentences just waiting to slither far away and completely out of your control.

So what's going on with long sentences? One problem is they're tiring to read. By the time readers reach the end of a long sentence, they've most likely forgotten the subject/verb/point of the sentence. And they're probably too tired or too lazy or too busy to go back to the beginning of the sentence and start over, to sort the whole thing out.

Another problem is long sentences lack punctuation. Punctuation is a big part of rhythm. The start and stop of a period. The bated breath of an em-dash. Think of punctuation as your percussion section.

But when you write a long sentence, all you have to work with is the quiet sigh of the unobtrusive comma. Yes, they have their place. But it's a subtler instrument. (Think triangle rather than kettledrum.)

A good rule of thumb is to make sure a single sentence doesn't go over 30 words. If it does, strongly consider breaking it in two. Or three.

2. **Vary sentence length.** In music, a steady beat is usually a good thing. In writing, it's considered one of the deadly sins. (Okay, not really. But it isn't good writing.)

If every sentence is the same length, your writing is going to get pretty dull pretty quickly. You need short sentences, longer sentences (but not too long) medium length sentences and very short sentences.

How do you know if your sentences are all the same? Does your piece sound monotonous? Are you getting a sing-song voice in your head when you read it? If so, you better take a closer look at those sentence lengths. They're probably all pretty close to being the same.

3. Consider using **sentence fragments.** Forget your fourth-grade English teacher. Forget that obnoxious green line in Microsoft Word telling you your grammar is wrong. In copywriting, as well as in many other forms of writing, sentence fragments are a lifesaver. Those fragments allow you to quickly and easily vary your sentence length. Plus, they can help your writing sound conversational. People talk in sentence fragments. Therefore, reading sentence fragments gives people the impression you're talking to them — in your own voice and your own style.

So what's a sentence fragment? A sentence that isn't complete. It's missing something — noun, verb, both. It's not a complete sentence.

Again, the tips above have hopefully inspired you to at least think about your writing rhythm.

Ready to improve it? Let's go!

WRITING EXERCISES — GET IN TOUCH WITH YOUR WRITING RHYTHM

Reading things out loud is a good way to start getting in touch with your writing rhythm. You may have heard of using this technique to find mistakes in your writing — and yes, it's a good way to discover errors you might have otherwise overlooked. But, this technique is also an excellent way to start getting to know your own unique rhythm.

Start by reading your own work out loud. If you've never done this before, try not to be too hard on yourself. Chances are you're going to discover all sorts of problems — including sentences that are too long and paragraphs where all the sentences are the same length. Make a note of what needs fixing as you read.

Then, once you fix the errors, read it out loud again.

Next, read the original, again. Listen to the difference. Even better, try to feel the difference — deep inside, in your gut. (Your gut is an excellent rhythm- sensor.)

You should also read things aloud from other authors, , and be sure to read a variety of writing — plays, novels, direct mail pieces, newspaper articles, websites, poems. Read bad writing and read writing that's so beautiful your knees buckle. Most importantly, listen to the rhythm while you're reading. How does it make you feel? More importantly, how does it make your gut feel? Your gut will never lie to you — learn to trust it.

ABOUT MICHELE PW

Considered one of the hottest direct response copywriters and marketing consultants in the industry today, Michele PW (Michele Pariza Wacek) has a reputation for crafting copy and creating online and offline marketing campaigns that get results.

Michele started writing professionally in 1992, working at agencies and on staff as a marketing/communication/writing specialist. In 1998, she started her business as a freelance copywriter.

But she quickly realized her vision was bigger than serving her clients as a one-woman-shop. In 2004, she began the transformation to building a copywriting company.

Two years later, her vision turned into reality. The Love-Based Copywriting and Marketing Company is the premiere direct response copywriting and marketing company today, catering to entrepreneurs and small business owners internationally, including the "Who's Who" of Internet Marketing.

In addition, Michele is also a national speaker and author and has completed two novels. She holds a double major in English and Communications from the University of Wisconsin-Madison. Currently she lives in the mountains of Prescott, Arizona with her husband Paul and her 2 dogs — border collie Nick and southern squirrel hunter Cassie.

Resources

Love-Based Copywriting Companion Workbook

I created this companion workbook to not only help you deepen your learning as you read through this book, but to also guide you in actually writing your marketing copy. You can download it for free here:

www.lovebasedcopywritingbook.com/workbook

Love-Based Copywriting Template

I've put together a love-based copywriting template to help you integrate love-based principles into your copy. You can download it for free here:

www.lovebasedcopywritingbook.com/template

"Love-Based Marketing"

Book by Susan Liddy — "Love-Based Marketing: The No Sell-Out, Copy-Out, Burn-Out Method to Attract Your Soul Mate Clients into Your Business"

www.SusanLiddy.com

Other books in the Love-Based Business Series

Love-Based Online Marketing: Campaigns to Grow a Business You Love AND That Loves You Back (Volume 3 in the Love-Based Business Series)
By Michele PW

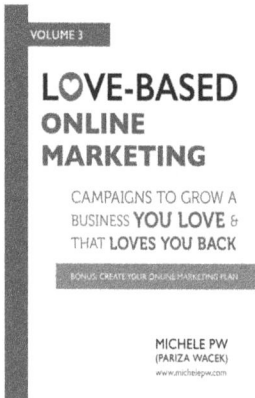

All successful, profitable businesses need a marketing plan, and this book walks you through how to create one that is perfect for you. You'll also learn the basics of selingl products and services online without feeling sales-y, and what might be standing in your way of successfully marketing your business.

lovebasedpublishing.com/book/love-based-online-marketing

Books 1 & 2

Love-Based Money and Mindset: Make the Money You Desire Without Selling Your Soul
(Volume 4 in the Love-Based Business Series)
By Michele PW

Are you ready to step into a life of peaceful prosperity? "Love-Based Money and Mindset" is designed to help you heal your relationship with money so you not only feel peaceful about it, but you're also able to attract all the abundance you want.

While this book is designed to help everyone who struggles with money issues, it's particularly helpful for those who have (or want to have) a business. The bottom line: the more you can cultivate a love-based mindset, the more easily and effortlessly you'll attract money into your life.

lovebasedpublishing.com/book/love-based-money-mindset

Love-Based Goals: Your Guide to Living Your Purpose & Passion
(Volume 5 in the Love-Based Business Series)
By Michele PW

VOLUME 5

LOVE-BASED GOALS

YOUR GUIDE
TO **LIVING**
YOUR **PURPOSE**
& **PASSION**

MICHELE PW
(PARIZA WACEK)

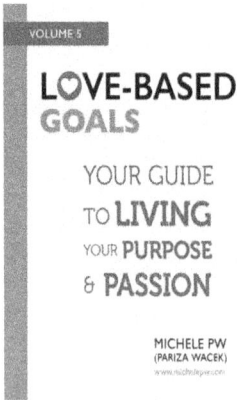

If you're ready to step into the life of your dreams and do it with ease and grace, this book can help. You'll get the tools you need to discover your love-based goals, get clear on what's stopping you and create an individualized plan to help you finally start living your dream life.

lovebasedpublishing.com/book/love-based-goals

Books 1 & 2

Love-Based Business Models: A Simple System For Bulding A Business You Love
(*Volume 6* in the Love-Based Business Series)
By Shawn Driscoll

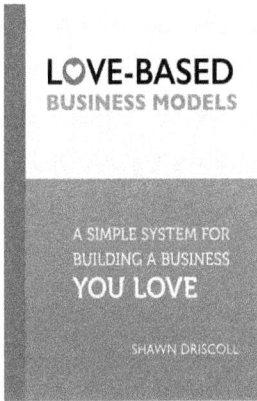

LOVE-BASED
BUSINESS MODELS

A SIMPLE SYSTEM FOR
BUILDING A BUSINESS
YOU LOVE

SHAWN DRISCOLL

In this book, Business Coach Shawn Driscoll teaches you the philosophy and the foundational principles behind creating business models that fit with and support your life, priorities, interests, demands, strengths, and weaknesses. Whether you're a seasoned entrepreneur or you're just starting out, you'll discover practical tips and strategies for identifying and building a business around your unique strengths and your mission, using a model that maximizes your impact and supports everything that's important to you.

lovebasedpublishing.com/book/business-models

Love-Based Mission :
How to Create a Business That Serves Your Soul
(Volume 7 in the Love-Based Business Series)
By Therese Skelly

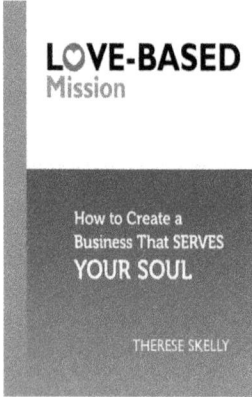

There is something specific that you and you alone are here to do for the world. It's your soul's purpose for your life. In Love-Based Mission, you'll uncover what holds you back and discover who you must be to birth your mission-driven business.

lovebasedpublishing.com/book/love-based-mission

How to Start a Business You Love AND That Loves You Back: Get Clear on Your Purpose & Passion - Build a Successful, Profitable Business
Part of the Love-Based Business Series
By Michele PW

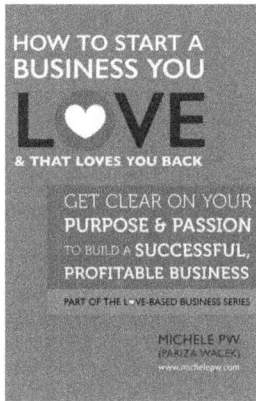

This book includes exercises and questions to ask yourself to make sure the heart of your business reflects what you really want it to. It's about answering the deeper questions around your business, like why you want it in the first place—because the clearer you are in your answers to those questions, the more satisfied you'll most likely be with what you eventually build.

Michele wrote this book for you if you don't have a business yet, but you want to get started, and you're intrigued by the idea of having a business you love and that loves you back.

Get it for FREE, here:

lovebasedpublishing.com/book/how-to-start-a-biz-you-love

DON'T WANT TO WRITE YOUR OWN COPY BUT STILL WANT IT TO BE LOVE-BASED?

WE WOULD BE HAPPY TO WRITE YOUR COPY FOR YOU!

DONE-FOR-YOU COPYWRITING SERVICES — GET MORE LEADS, CLIENTS AND SALES WITHOUT DOING THE WORK YOURSELF!

As a busy entrepreneur or small business owner, you're probably looking for ways to leverage your time and money. Well, there's no better leverage than direct response copywriting.

Consider this — copywriting leverages your marketing and your selling. You can make money without picking up the phone and selling one-on-one. (Imagine the time saving right there.) You can easily add multiple streams of income to your business. You can turn your website into a lead-generation tool so you have a consistently full pipeline of clients. You can send out an email or a direct mail piece and watch money flow into your business!

That's the beauty of direct response copywriting.

But there's only one small problem — if you want results, you need to be trained. And, as a busy entrepreneur or small business owner, who has time for training?

That's why I'd like to introduce you to the Michele PW Done-For-You Copywriting Services. Whether you're looking for a one-shot copy project (like getting your website written or a few emails or a postcard) or an entire project launch campaign, or a combination of copywriting and marketing strategy, our team of trained copywriters and marketing strategists can take care of your needs and (even more importantly) get you the results you're looking for.

Want to learn more? Just email or call for the details — Info@MichelePW.com or (toll free) 877-754-3384 X2.

(Note — we also write articles, press releases, social networking posts and more.
Just ask if you want to learn more.)

TESTIMONIALS

"Working with Michele PW was such a relief because she GETS direct response copywriting. She knew what I was looking for and was able to deliver. With her help, we had record-breaking numbers for one of our campaigns. I highly recommend Michele if you're looking for copywriting that gets you results."

Ali Brown
Founder of Alexandria Brown International
www.AlexandriaBrown.com

"With Michele's copywriting and social networking help, I had my BIGGEST 6-figure launch ever! And I'm no stranger to 6-figure product launches. Before Michele, I had 5 6-figure launches. But this one I did with Michele blew all the other ones away. We more than doubled what I had done before. Plus, even though I knew the launch was on track, there were moments I panicked because I wasn't staying up until 2 a.m. writing copy. I highly recommend Michele, especially if you're getting ready to launch a new product or service."

Lisa Sasevich
The Queen of Sales Conversion
www.LisaSasevich.com

"I've had the pleasure of working with some of the top marketing minds of our time, and as far as results are concerned, Michele is right there with them. One idea she gave me for one of my recent launches, directly resulted in a 30% increase of sales. I'm planning on implementing that idea on a regular basis the results were so powerful. Thanks Michele!"

Mark Harris
Co-Founder www.ThoughtLeaderSecrets.com

"With Michele's expert copywriting and marketing help, we're averaging an 8% conversion rate! Considering that 1% is typically considered really good by industry standards, we were blown away by the results."

Linda H. Hunt
Owner
www.sumsolutions.com

"Thanks to your eagle eye and copywriting changes to ONE simple email I increased registrations for my "Give Your Pricing a Kick-in-the-Pants" Virtual Workshop Intensive by 20%! That's money that went straight into my bank account!"

Kendall SummerHawk
The "Horse Whisperer for Business"
Author, "How to Charge What You're Worth and Get It!"
www.KendallSummerHawk.com

www.ingramcontent.com/pod-product-compliance
Lightning Source LLC
Chambersburg PA
CBHW071335210326
41597CB00015B/1458